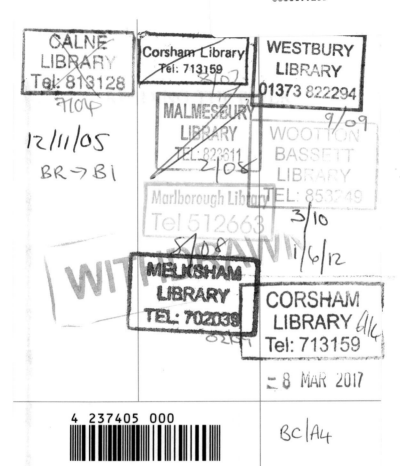
This book may be returned to any Wiltshire
library. To renew this book phone your library
or visit the website: www.wiltshire.gov.uk

Wiltshire
COUNTY COUNCIL

CHILDREN, EDUCATION & LIBRARIES

LM6.108.5

Books by Robert Adamson

POETRY

Canticles on the Skin 1970

The Rumour 1971

Swamp Riddles 1974

Theatre 1975

Cross the Border 1977

Selected Poems 1977

Where I Come From 1979

The Law at Heart's Desire 1982

The Clean Dark 1989

Selected Poems 1970–1989

The Brutality of Fact 1993

Waving to Hart Crane 1994

The Language of Oysters
   with photography by Juno Gemes 1997

Meaning 1999

Black Water: Approaching Zukofsky 1999

Mulberry Leaves: New & Selected Poems 1970–2001 2001

Reading the River: Selected Poems 2004

AUTOBIOGRAPHICAL FICTION

Zimmer's Essay (with Bruce Hanford) 1974

Wards of the State 1990

AUTOBIOGRAPHY

Inside Out 2004

ROBERT ADAMSON

Reading the River

SELECTED POEMS

BLOODAXE BOOKS

Copyright © Robert Adamson 1970, 1971, 1974, 1975, 1977,
1979, 1982, 1989, 1990, 1994, 1997, 1998, 1999, 2001, 2004

ISBN: 1 85224 639 1

First published 2004 by
Bloodaxe Books Ltd,
Highgreen,
Tarset,
Northumberland NE48 1RP.

www.bloodaxebooks.com
For further information about Bloodaxe titles
please visit our website or write to
the above address for a catalogue.

Bloodaxe Books Ltd acknowledges
the financial assistance of
Arts Council England, North East.

ARTS COUNCIL ENGLAND

Wiltshire Libraries & Heritage	
Askews	
821.92	£10.95

Cover printing by J. Thomson Colour Printers Ltd, Glasgow.

Printed in Great Britain by
Cromwell Press Ltd, Trowbridge, Wiltshire.

This book is for Juno

ACKNOWLEDGEMENTS

This first UK edition of Robert Adamson's poetry is largely drawn from *Mulberry Leaves: New & Selected Poems 1970-2001* (Paper Bark Press, 2001). It includes a larger selection from *Black Water: Approaching Zukofsky* (Brandl & Schlesinger, 1999), with the poems in their original order but using the 2001 texts for any revised poems.

Grateful acknowledgement is also made to the editors and publishers of earlier books represented in this selection: *Canticles on the Skin* (Illumination Press, 1970), *The Rumour* (Prism Books, 1971), *Swamp Riddles* (Island Press, 1974), *Theatre* (Pluralist Press, 1975), *Cross the Border* (Prism Books, 1977), *Where I Come From* (Big Smoke Books, 1979), *The Law at Heart's Desire* (Prism Books, 1982), *The Clean Dark* (Paper Bark Press, 1989), *Wards of the State* (Harper-Collins Imprint 1990), *Waving to Hart Crane* (Angus & Robertson/ Harper Collins, 1994), *The Language of Oysters* (Craftsman Press, 1997) and *Meaning* (Poetical Histories Series, no. 46, Cambridge, 1998).

Grateful acknowledgement is also made to the editors and publishers of publications in which some of new poems (1999-2001) from *Mulberry Leaves* first appeared: *The Age, Atlanta Review* (USA), *The Australian, Boxkite, Chicago Review* (USA), *Cordite, Heat, Imago, Island Magazine, Kenyon Review* (USA), *Malahat Review* (Canada), *Meanjin, Newcastle Poetry Prize Anthology 1999, Overland, Picador New Writing, Poetry Review* (UK), *Prism* (Canada), *Salt, Southerly, Southern Review* (USA), *Stand* (UK), *Sydney Morning Herald.*

The author would like to acknowledge the generous support of the Literature Board of the Australia Council during the composition of this book. Grateful acknowledgment is made to the Literature Board of the Australia Council and to the Cambridge Conference of Contemporary Poetry for funding the author's attendance at the Conference at Trinity College in 1998, and to the Australia Council for funding his visit to the UK and Ireland in 2004. Thanks are also due to Chris Edwards for his editorial and technical advice.

CONTENTS

New Poems (2004)

FOREWORD

In one of the more recent poems in this rich selection ('On not see-
ing Paul Cézanne'), Robert Adamson writes:

> Everything that matters comes together
> slowly, the hard way, with the immense and tiny details,
> all the infinite touches, put down onto nothing –

We need to acknowledge the full weight of that 'nothing' – nihil-
ism has always been a strong temptation in Adamson's work. But
so has what he sets against it: the world as experience – everything
that, in its separateness and wholeness, matters – all those touches
of the infinite that, as Blake saw, are in the smallest as well as the
largest phenomena. We also need to acknowledge the full weight of
the word 'slowly'. The shining immediacy of the moment is one
thing. What comes only with time is another. In the earliest poem
printed here, 'The rebel angel', the youthful ex-con's project is to
break out and discover (that is, make for himself) 'some kind of
law'. These poems are the thirty-year record of that making.

The tutelary deities that in Adamson's world make up a kind
of collective Muse – Shelley, Stevens, Mallarmé, Robert Duncan –
are all poets for whom the world as idea is embodied in the world
as language, for whom immense and tiny details, real objects in an
apprehensible and particular form, are doors that open directly
into mind, and an order there that has the shape of poetry. For
Adamson too poetry is simply the most immediate form of thinking
and being. For all his deliberate shifts and evasions, his playful
and sometimes wilful self-dramatisation in the role of 'rebel' – as
thief, con, hood, latter-day Autolycus son of Hermes, 'homosexual',
street-smart Adonais, conductor of lightning or conductor of the
inner music of things – he has remained, for more than thirty years
now, dedicated to the single task of bringing a chaotic world, and
what is in some ways an anarchic sensibility within the order of
words and music.

The subjects, the 'shining incidents' Adamson is drawn to, and
whose mystery he sets himself to fathom over and over again, are
few: prison in all its versions, and the many ways of 'breaking out';
the world of birds, and of fish and fishing; the light, tides and
seasons of 'his' river, the Hawkesbury; the 'trammel of lives', as
he puts it in one of the earliest poems, that binds him to family;
the crooked business of loving. What is impressive is the extent to
which each return, each revisiting of a familiar scene, yields a fresh
view, a renewed lyric order.

The spareness and taut energy of the more recent poems, for all
Adamson's famous romanticism, seems classic; as if, like Yeats, he
had discovered the exhilaration and enterprise of walking naked.

What it costs a poet to dare such plain statement, the patience it requires, even in impatience, the dedication, the hard work, is part of the mystery of these poems and of the life that has been worked through to get them down. Going along with Adamson as he does it is a more dramatic experience than even a poem like 'The rebel angel' might prepare us for, and more perhaps than Adamson himself was expecting. How the poems, as they come, change and shape the poet – the existential surprise that keeps him alive and on his toes – is what keeps us too, as we move through this life in poetry, intimately engaged and enlivened from first poem to last.

DAVID MALOUF

from

CANTICLES ON THE SKIN

(1970)

The rebel angel

Shit off with this fake dome of a life, why
    should I remain here locked in my own
buckling cells? So there's always
    a way round the city mornings when parks
are lakes of smouldering green –
    & there's a way as you're blown along
by some great vision of a cop
    who keeps farting inside your gut –
& you know so well the way that'll carry you back:
    follow a railway line

that's studded with muck-green stations
    & bubblers spouting lukewarm water – No,
you've left it too late & now there's
    cold weather coming along & that
pile of junk in your brain – These days it's
    risky to drive after midnight.
It's slowing you down always looking behind
    all the time getting someone to pluck
down the blinds – So now as you spin
    through a drunk there's lots of reasons
you have to stay put – reasons that say
    you can't piss off anymore from the calm
of serving two and a half years: of knowing
    it's lights out at ten every night, of knowing
the sleepless lays churning in your bunk
    until each counted dawn, of singing
without sound – I've looked around every inch
    of the jail & dug my own groove in yellow
sandstone, & searched without sleep
    & searched again

back on the street in the rain – searched for
    some kind of rebel angel,
    some kind of law.

Demimondane

Down along my mirror-sided town
I walk circular

madhouse boards, a somnambulist with
tall arms outstretched.

Something's wrong.
My fist has caged her face, snatched

at midnight from carbeams
on a loving place.

She slashed her wrist.
The hoods have bounced her like

a ball against green as aniseed
public halls.

She's no good. Though these days
she's mostly mine

while cruising in my Customline –
I find no fault in her

to praise – Her hair, her bucking mane?
what lair could I invent

to blotch this perfect blondness?
What lair, however sinister –

Her fingers snap against my heart,
her shallow eyes

search my art: her trap.

Through a trammel of lives

The delta of his years holds only time: each
night pursuing memories of place, he returns
to Jerusalem, his trawler's motor quiet now
as he travels the breaking Galilee of his age –
my grandfather, still at the rudder.

Three generations ago he took
to the Hawkesbury. Blood cold as fishes'
he lived right on the river, while his wife camped
in a lean-to he'd built for nets on the shore.
They say his first son was born
in a sandfly cloud one morning on the floor.
The daughter worked a smoke-house for his mullet
and never married.

I watch him at the stern of his boat
feeding out mesh, the corkline hissing softly, floating
across heaven, and his leadline dragging
the silt of hell – I come astern
dripping, with my end of tackle snared up.
His hands grip my wrists, guiding in rope.

He rides alone on the stern, feeling for knots
in the fine nylon chords. I am fixed
to the net-board by the spike
of his will – And his old motor's thumping along
as soft as a heart as we glide beneath branches
of mangrove in four feet of water.
And his catch still alive
slung over the trawler's green side.

Toward abstraction / possibly a gull's wing

The most disconcerting feature is an absolue flatness
especially the sand. I've been here in love
and having passed the perfectly calm ocean had only
noticed the terns – If there was some way
back, some winding track to follow I'd possibly find
the elusive creative agents.

As now for instance, I am completely indifferent
to the sad way that fellow moves over the sand... Who?
Let's be pure in observation, let's drop opinions –
Look: he stops and, throwing off his towel,
runs into the surf, where stroking out he attracts the terns
that begin to curve above him.

Now look back to the beach. It is mid-winter.
The sand's deserted and eddies of windcaught grit are left
to dance and fall unhindered. At the far end of the beach
is an object – a rifle, rusting. He comes out from
the surf, stubbing his toes, heading towards the place
where the rifle lies melting.

The sand whispers beneath his feet as he passes by the gun.
Dazed, he goes in no particular direction.
The surf rolls a dead tern onto the sand and he kicks it.
Its wings unfold like a fan, sealice fall from the sepia
feathers and the feathers take flight.

from

THE RUMOUR

(1971)

Action would kill it / a gamble

When I couldn't he always discussed things.
His talk drew us together:
the government's new war, the best French brandies
and breaking the laws. And it seemed
a strange thing for us to be doing,
the surf right up the beach, wetting our
feet each wave

on that isolated part of the coast, counting over
the youngest politicians.
Huge shoulders of granite grew higher
as we walked on, cutting us from perspectives.
He swung his arms and kicked
lumps of quartz hard with bare feet,
until I asked him to stop it...

He didn't care about himself at all, and the sea
just licked his blood away.
The seemingly endless beach held us firm;
we walked and walked all day
until it was dark. The wind dropped off and the surf
flattened out, as silence grew round
us in the darkness.

We moved on, close together, almost touching.
He wouldn't have noticed; our
walk covered time rather than distance.
When the beach ended,
we would have to split up. And as he spoke
clearly and without emotion
about the need for action, about killing people,
I wanted him.

The unpopular scale of values

I

Why should I ever use the word Owl when it rubs
Against the grain? The bird
Itself works by chemicals also   Owls have
Been used over

II

And over I shall not use the word or the word's
Meaning it seems both are very
Acceptable

III

O juventes, O filu, O Stevens
A traditional poem about an owl could be a windy
Thing

IV

I am not a humble man

V

Working with my hands doesn't justify my poetry
As far as writing's concerned
It's one or the other

VI

Did stanza three seem 'a bit much'? it is
Not really serious

VII

Owls are easy to use in a
Serious poem because they fly by night   The word's
Been on my mind all week   Stanza
Two's a lie

Passing through experiences

I lived on drugs and understood the pushers
As the crackup came on
There was nobody to blame and I confessed for hours
Until the police were in tears

The prison had a few prophets but they
Understood themselves
During the night the lucky ones burnt their tobacco
Each morning I feigned silence

The experience of prison remained behind bars
I dwelt on the idea of freedom
And folding *The Prince* away when afternoon appeared
Went after pain

The ideas crowded around like pushers
And fed on my doings
I discovered thought as powerful as cocaine in winter
As a screw off duty I tapped my foot

All experience pointed to Saint Theresa
The Prince reassured me
I escaped from the books but names kept coming up
Pain alone said nothing great

I ask her *why you know it all though say nothing*
Believe me pain replies *You don't falter*
You move

The domesticity

She drove out the moisture and the long dust
of three years   she wanted to
move unencumbered   running nameless
but domesticity gathered in

its wings and wouldn't move   squatting before
each step she made away   She
closed her eyes and pushed outwards
then her fists were

opened to moist palms that caressed
the domesticity   She overwhelmed it with raw desire
until it left her to fume
at the washing–up   She tried biting

her hand everything turned to sex
She called through the hours to domesticity
but it slept alone   She
smashed the bed her mirror and the washing-up

ran into the side alley with bare feet
that bleeding left pad-marks
When she had no food she ate scraps   slept in parks
running nameless

until she could stand it no longer
then as a prostitute   domesticity came to her
throwing her into bed with nightly clean sheets
using her well   paying her rent

paying her back

A revelation

Whatever I see this morning
is important a day
for changing my mind nothing can
really be altered outside
in the bush
something on sandy ground happens
and is gone in an instant now
a mating bird perhaps
what it was
or will be again can't be tampered with
today my succession
of goddesses have worn
themselves into – moving feathers?
It could've been
anything maybe something
that had nothing to do with me

Card tables covered with dice

Why it has to be in any direction I don't know
I live in a space that travels
Some look up   but many of those around me
Look down   yet others

Watch what they think is my life
From eye level or look over their shoulders
Imagining that's my place
Possibly they all know my whereabouts

I never jump to conclusions the mind can only take
So much before accomplishing
Silence   The dice-throwers of thought are
Seeking my direction

You can hear cards whispering on the green baize
Chinese gangsters at poker
Their gloves covered in red ink

The games are not in my life any more
I live wherever I can
Often feeling my way through calendars blindly

Getting further away

(for John Tranter)

I

there is always a point when suddenly
we stand to gain some news mostly it passes
quickly and we don't understand
we have lost everything
it is a point when to persist could mean losing
our grip on sanity
so we let up and the news from inside is
trapped there swelling

II

and winds outside blowing about your head carry
different sounds with them
that enter the body mingle and disperse
in the brain until
they are inseparable like radio
signals coming from a war where the enemy is
also broadcasting in english
brain cells

III

are not constantly dying as decadent ministers
they decipher the sounds into news
for the willpower the spirit
rushes around like a puritan at the point
when we stand to gain
everything the news offers the realistic
willpower fans out to patrol our gushing
filaments of adrenaline

IV

only when the will breaks
news is released, only when the puritan spirit
escapes

SWAMP RIDDLES

(1974)

Things going out of my life

The things that are going out of my life remain
in its wake a few yards

behind following me asking to be retrieved like
cigarette packets bobbing
at the stern of a boat leaving
with the tide

And it seldom occurs to me that they are not in
the water but could be falling
from my life

as it rises up from earth
or tumbling haphazardly downhill after me
These things leaving

often ask to be identified even though they know
it would be impossible

When I wake up mornings alone it is more disturbing
when I imagine it could be
the living things
that are going out of my life

Sibyl

Then with my white sails and bad luck
with the wind I am beautiful
each dawn there is more resentment towards me fishermen
cannot look as the sun
catches my hair turning spokes
on their decks

So again I depart from the side of the planet
the boy who sleeps with me
Why speak

Goshawk over Broken Bay

Pale morning grows through mist, settles on the bay
And lifts a hawk into the chilly air.
Warm inside my house I lean back on a chair,
Gaze through frosty windows at midwinter's grey.

A lone fisherman walks the rocky shore.
The hawk hovers, white, on a breeze above the beach:
Winter ghost-wings, out beyond my reach.
I check a field guide as sunlight moves over the floor

And meets the grate of my electric fire.
The man and bird are fishing from the headland's reef:
Seen through glass, distortions of my grief
Kindle the flames of a theatrical desire.

The hawk tumbles for its balance in a pocket of air.
I hold the bird book tightly in my hands.
My whole life seems curbed by these demands
For order – I fling back the chair,

Stride straight through the back door to the high
Verandah and stare directly at the hawk.
There is no order: just excuses for more talk.
I turn, instead of jumping from the rail I sigh –

Sonnets to be written from prison

(for James Tulip)

1

O to be 'in the news' again – now as fashion runs
everything would go for 'prison sonnets': I'd be on my own.
I could, once more, go out with pale skin
from my veritable dank cell – the sufferer, poking fun
at myself in form, with a slightly twisted tone.
My stance, ironic – one-out, on the run.
Though how can I? I'm not locked up: imagine a typewriter
in solitary. I dream my police unable to surrender –
I'm bored with switching roles and playing
with my gender; the ironies seem incidental, growing thin.
Here's the world – maybe what's left of it –
held together by an almost experimental sonnet.
Surely there must be some way out of poetry other than
Mallarmé's: still-life with bars and shitcan.

2

Once more, almost a joke – this most serious endeavour
is too intense: imagine a solitary typewriter? Somehow
fashion runs its course: I am not in pain,
so there's hardly any need to play on abstract repetitions
to satisfy a predecessor, poet or lawbreaker. I won't be clever –
all the clever crims are not inside the prisons.
Here's the world – maybe what's left of my pretences:
I dream of being carried off to court again,
a sufferer, where all my deities would speak in stern
almost sardonic voices: 'Your Honour, please,
bring me to my senses.' There, I love confessions –
imagine writing prison sonnets four years after my release.
If only all my memories could be made taciturn
by inventing phrases like: imagine the solitary police.

3

Yes your Honour, I know this is ridiculous – although
I'm 'in the news'. I couldn't bring myself to do
one of those victimless crimes: I must suffer in more ways
than one. My crime's pretence is not to overthrow
social order, or to protest – it's my plan
to bring poetry and lawbreaking into serious interplay.
Imagine newspapers in solitary. I would walk right through
the court taking down copy – 'catch me if you can' –
Defendant in contempt. There has to be a fight,
I can't imagine anything if I'm not up against a law.
Here's the world – our country's first stone institution –
where inmates still abase themselves each night.
If I was in solitary I could dream – a fashionable bore,
writing books on drugs, birds or revolution.

4

I dreamed I saw the morning editions settle on the court
emblazoned with my name, my 'story' so glib it made
no sense. The judge said 'emotional' but I thought
of the notoriety. This was the outward world and my sad tirade
was news – Though if I'd been rhyming sonnets
in solitary, my suffering alone could've make them art.
Now, imagine an illiterate in prison – but I have no regrets,
I enjoy my laggings. I feel sorry for the warders.
The discipline always pulls me through, and my counterpart,
the screw, is tougher with the easy boarders –
This experience might feel profound, but irony's never
broken laws – so I'm against everything
but practical intuitions. My 'solitary etc.' is too clever
by half now – but then, who's suffering?

5

I brood in solitary, it's a way to flagellation: thinking
of my 'day of release' – I shuffle friends like dates
on my calendar, marking them off at random.
Here's the world – the stewed tea I'm drinking
cold – how I suffer. When I walk through the front gates
into the country, what will I become?
I'll throw away the sufferer's comforting mask
and turn against my memories, leaving a trail of perdition
behind me. Children and women will fall to my simple
intuitive reactions – not even the New Journalists will ask
questions, nothing will be able to feed on
my actions and survive. My prison sonnets will be drugs
relieving pain: I have remembered helpless men
knocking their bars for hours with aluminium mugs –

6

We will take it seriously as we open our morning paper.
Someone's broken loose, another child's been
wounded by penknives. A small fire down the bottom
of a suburban garden smells of flesh. Dark circles under
the mother's eyes appear on television, she's seen
her baby at the morgue. Our country moves closer to the world:
a negro's book is on the shelves. The criminal's become
mythologised, though yesterday he curled
over and didn't make the news. So the myth continues, growing
fat and dangerous on a thousand impractical intuitions.
The bodies of old sharks hang on the butcher's hooks.
In broad daylight somewhere a prisoner is escaping.
The geriatrics are floating in their institutions.
The myth is torn apart and stashed away in books.

The beautiful season

Some sunny day does not support any more
reason than a dull one; green lights
from the harbour still remind us of a tour
through Spain. Two whistling-kites

are fishing in a shallow day: even birds
would not support a proper reason
for the inclusion of corroborated words.
A sample of the beautiful season

came wrapped in aluminium foil: oh cute
as a new drug – but let's remember
how the most vicious thug wore silk suits
and plugged sparrows in December.

The sunny day is no more 'cute' than a drug
in foil; lights on water are seldom
memories. Our bird-loving thug
has returned muttering 'O Kingdoms'

Some more experiences

Seems we were born in captivity, he said, and burn
Our curious lives out in these slow states
Numbered by the days; who knows? My lover's turn-
Coat mind turns about, dreaming of the gates.

And he forgets me easily behind the yellow walls.
He's been round on the outer – screws
Tell me he's even got a wife who calls
The Commissioner every day for some news

Of his release. (As if they'd know –
They bitch me many ways.) All night he talks
And holds me, all night he loves me slow
And careful. The screws pace the catwalks –

In time their footsteps mark our love.
Who, now, can really know him more than me?
Once he hugged me till my bones were sore –
We understood the terror then in being free.

Seems we should be born in captivity, I said; love
Might hold our curious lives in some new lore.
Oh, yeah, he said, whatever you reckon –
Love's a laggin' in a way, whatever you reckon.

Wind without flags

This is another one of my lies.
I say to myself, homosexual –
it hardly matters these days, when
I go to the local park utterly
bemused by white lies I stumble on
no desire, desire to hunt comes

from the shock. Between midnight
and dawn often I go back, only
to find those sentimental girls who
once wanted to marry me: they
have forgotten now, though would
die of fear if they only knew
what I have made of them. Some

things are meant to last, I tell
myself, some things I say to myself.
There is the kite high again
swinging on the breeze: brown paper
sign held to the field by some
kid. I walk back, sure of my way

now, I walk back naming the pigeons:
Blue Bar, Checker, Flighty –
O my sad road-peckers.

Sail away

Our day was composed of resemblances. Take
the heavy cloudbank as a mountain, as it lifted
itself up from behind the headland: how

its appearance altered to disintegrating
fluxive streaks as we spoke. We were sitting quietly
by the river as the colours changed.

And as we spoke – however gingerly – we knew
the blackbird in our voice, and watched it flying
there, high above the water, until our

conversation resembled its elusive song –
though it was the bird that sang amidst the rolls
of thunder and, as we listened, its notes

rose and fell around us on the ridiculous earth:
so that all we really saw was in the sky
of that electric evening. Maybe it was summer

and it was summer's shifting colours
through which our blackbird tumbled, as if evening
was not an imagined time: so in the orange

atmosphere the blackbird darted from my voice
to yours, and we almost held each other by the hand.
A breeze ran along the surface as if it was

a breeze, and the surface of the river
kicked against it, as if there was a tide coming in.
The blackbird sang as if it had a song.

The crossing

(for Cheryl)

Below full tide the catfish swim
long dark ribbons moving

slowly over the empty oysters –
From the house, where you

are waiting up, a clock's moving
against me – Only hours apart

and mathematics divide us.
When I return and hold you again

finally there will be sleep;
just to stroke your hair

and the coldest planet would relent.
Then we will watch the sun rise

washing the night's work
from my eyes, outshining

the sharp morning star: awaking
we'll see ourselves again,

and taste the brackish river on
our lips: full morning

will soothe storms in your eyes,
as I tried during the night.

Though what can I offer? you,
from another river, what desire?

I have never tried to bless you:
though have wanted you here

each night, as the crossings bless
me – the river difficult

to navigate, and the tides
against me with a terrible patience.

I belong to you, now let nothing
divide us, even this.

The shining incidents

1 *A new legend*

In a friendless time the mind swims
out from its body: you become
all the lives you have ever lived.
In this clearing there have
been camp fires, though the ashes
are stone cold now. And the mist
just above the earth is
undisturbed. A brown kestrel flits

between the sun and the ancient
dwellings, its shadow a moth
wandering below the mist's surface.
Everything has been like this
for centuries. Sunlight struggles
through onto the petrified
branches of charcoal; as I walk
I create a new legend here –

my voice moves over the rock carvings,
my hands net for the moth's
faint dancing shadow, my eyes
vanish into the back of my head
and a small creature stops running.
The water lies still in granite
waiting for the chance to sing anew;
under the mist I become

a thousand echoes, sounding for
the time being. Wherever life emanates
it's born from my careful presence
here, treading: mushrooms bloom
in my footsteps among the ashes.
The mind moves ahead of my
body now, feeling the new wings,
wondering if they existed before.

Its thoughts lift me above the ground.
I look down at my body, a feeble
creature moving through its own silence.
Moss clings to my thighs, the kestrel
dives into the clearing hooking
up the creature I taught not to fear.

2 *Drifting through silence*

Again she returns to me, in grey
morning, a complete woman.
The swamp is merely breaking in
her memory of another life: once
more her warmth rushes along
the filaments of my spirit. God,
where on earth are we travelling?
Huge wings unfold against

the earth, a breeze ruffles our
feathers as we move now
like native companions: the arrogant
brolga leaps amongst old stumps
of mangrove branches. When we
learnt to fly, we danced wildly in
the shadow of a new tree. Her
blood goes pulsing through tiny

constellations in my eyes: logic
says, impossible, impossible!
The bird leads us on, our planet's
drifting through silence without an
atmosphere of its own: we are
creating humming auroras, damp fern
grows up from the desert. Our
hearts beat of their own accord,

the stars come out from their pale
reflections, circling our heads,
I watch massive mangrove swamps rise
above the earth, the sun slowly
drying sap from their roots – a clear
river runs through the sky, empty
shells sing like kingfishers.
A new butterfly sails through a rain

storm – My love's voice sets out
for the throat of the nearest bird –
I call for more singing, she
sings less. An extinct night parrot
calls; we hear fugues impossible to
perform sound under dead water.

3 *The night parrots*

A song rose from thickets, your
song, continuing beyond warbling
catbirds. I had nothing to do
with it, wilderness came hurtling
toward me and I backed off, standing
still as a redwood with fear.
All my feelings rushed away, love
joined the skeletons of gentle

night parrots. A slovenly explorer
broke through swamps, terrified –
shooting wild animals, even though
his supplies were holding out.
He didn't bother eating the game;
the timid numbats were knocked into
undergrowth, bullets between
their eyes. Shale flaked from a

mountainside turning to grey sands,
I heard the sound of my love on the
verge of starvation: her song
spent on marsh water. She came for
my love that had turned to bone,
I simply watched. A mangrove tree,
centuries old, grew out from her heart,
its roots twining through her

body, feeding on her feeble spirit –
My mind rose above it all, observing
this from a distance. She wandered
into a swamp and slept on dead waters;
prawns began feeding on her undersides –
silence carried her spirit to the
tiny body of a kingfisher. King tides
flooded the swamp, covering

the whole myth with shining blue water.
The explorer struggles onto a shore
of grey sands, his men blasting away
at the shadows of teal and the spirits
of geese. He finally breaks camp,
under the skeletons of night parrots.

4 *The ghost crabs*

I flow back into myself with tide.
O moon that draws us and drives
us and we move through until we are
dancing. Balancing starlight on
the marshes, shaking the leaves
or calming the water. Feeling warmth,
ghost crabs come out, their claws
snapping held high in the air.

The river pulls at mangrove roots
as the ebb begins: standing to
my waist in water, prawns kick up
from under my toes – My love
would have me go now – moving off
with the river, skidding along
beneath the silt, head filled with
water. Now flexing my limbs,

the shock of feeling comes back
to my nerves: memories play
their part again. Swamp flowers are
opening, ready for sunlight,
vines twine closer to their branches
and a kingfisher ruffles its feathers
against the dew. She beckons from
the far shore, a chill runs

along my arms – I wade into shallows
calling, and straining my sight.
She moves there through the mist,
dancing and calling softly, hardly
moving the vegetation. My hands
shoot out over the tide, gleaming as
fish in a soft light. The senses
strain forward towards claws

turning and growing from the dawn.
I cannot reach, hands drift
down through the moonlight onto the
outgoing tide. Morning surrounds
me silently, sun hitting driftwood,
dead roots and branches.

Berowra Waters

In small skiffs before dawn fishermen came
through the valley sliding over calm waters.
Thinking of their catch, the long silver
ribbonfish, I stooped carefully over
the river from a rotting jetty into silence
and mist. Campaigns rose from reflected stars,
our campaigns against the flags of heaven:
murder of sacred fishes, the destruction of trees.
Then I rose from my reflection also
heroic in silver victory – and on the jetty
my catch, white as the planets and shining there
as inconstant as prayer.

from

CROSS THE BORDER

(1977)

Lovesong from across the border

I drive, so all I've taken in
revolving here will be turned about
change and drift freely across the border
and there dissolve; from transformations
no reassuring sign or moment
caught by memory. Though
every various instant spark
and disrupt the moving song
I'm only aware of what comes before
as I plunge through the life I burn.
I drive, and the lawless music I make
clears the air, moving in no direction,
is a swift flame dancing, and is alive
with the energies separating words.
Driven in fear, driven in love,
all instincts awake, I drive
the complete body now
so consciousness is forced to follow
out beyond order, language adrift,
exploding, moving through, and
taking me forward from there.

Parrot poem

There is a parrot drawn all from rainbows –
remember its name? – a bird caught
briefly in crossing sunlight.

Where does the parrot end and the poem
start? Drop the philology,
take this chance

to write directly from emotion. Close
the book and get it straight, push through
to what you think you see –

the parrot
glides between eye and brain,
a sentiment arising

through your skin, a streak in the sky,
through branches breaking in sun's white,
a smear of light

travelling into deep skull. A flock
of rainbow lorikeets passing through
lungs, eyes, memory –

hereby recorded
as they fly

Dead Horse Bay

Quick hands on spinning ropes
at dawn, blood rising
to the jumping cords,

ice-packs over bad burns
and the catfish venom,
rock salt against gut-slime,

a southerly blowing up
on the full tide, nets
in mud and mesh-gutting snags,

the bread tasting
like kero-sponge, crazed gulls
crashing onto the stern

and mullet at 3 cents a pound
by the time the sun hits the bar
at the Angler's Rest.

Get drunk enough to keep at it,
clean the gear for tonight
and another bash.

Remember that night in '68
how we killed 'em
right through the month

couldn't have gone wrong,
so thick you could've
walked over the water.

When the bream are running
like that, nothing can touch you
and everything matters

and you don't want 'em to stop
and you can't slow down
you can't imagine.

The river

A step taken, and all the world's before me.
The night's so clear

stars hang in the low branches,
small fires riding through the waves of a thin atmosphere,

islands parting tides as meteors burn the air.
Oysters powder to chalk in my hands.

A flying fox swims by and an early
memory unfolds: rocks

on the shoreline milling the star-fire.
Its fragments fall into place, the heavens

revealing themselves
as my roots trail

deep nets between channel and
shoal, gathering in

the Milky Way, Gemini –
I look all about, I search all around me.

There's a gale in my hair as the mountains move in.
I drift over lakes, through surf breaks

and valleys, entangled of trees –
unseemly? *On the edge or place inverted*

from Ocean starts another place,
its own place –

a step back and my love's before me,
the memory ash – we face each other alone now,

we turn in the rushing tide again and again to each other,
here between swamp-flower and star

to let love go forth to the world's end
to set our lives at the centre

though the tide turns the river back on itself
and at its mouth, Ocean.

Apprehensions

I fell away   savaging my prey there
                    a psyche in division
         tore birds from the sky   to feed my spirit
had fishermen up
        and out in gales on the wrong tide
             My life seemed part by particle
          indivisible
          with Life   Time
warping the seasons   changing continuously within
     at twilight hunting with sleek hawks
            their killing forming
               veils between
   my heart and mind
my other sex   an animal interlocutor
      who bore dream away
            white speed   out
a surge   from teenage apprehensions
   up from the spirit of earth
out from the river
   fucking mortals
         leading souls away from grief
            until they were led astray
        taunting the spirits
     shifting my body
        mingling with the filaments of
   the underground   then breaking back
into sun   a feline   daimon   conscience
   cat-attendant

      my eyes   the colour of falcons'

Sunlight, moonlight

Out of a dying out of a death a new life shoots
Tide's deeper tension singing under the sapwood rockers
Sunlight through the smokehouse smoulders
Dry ice under canvas   mould eats the boathouse chaff bags
There's a familiar smell   of tar on the breeze
And the winter mullet too early in the season
Always slow and always now
The punishing fear of isolation
Winter nights dark with Eros taunting in the form of
Ribbonfish dancing   away within a tempest
And native doves   tumbling   swung
By fire and harsh summer   through these
Ancient signatures on rock

With each thing energy with each object each one
With the power to change
Energy the sunlight energy the panic
In doves in branches energy
And from the eyes

It was the river gathering in throughout
My forming limbs a feline sense
That tore down sexual boundaries in that
Separating light

I knew quicksilver and the darker water birds
And showered at the base of a mountain
Where water fell through mangroves

Winter warmed my nakedness
Seasons passed within my passing year
Cold desires rapt my heart and I bore twin anima

WHERE I COME FROM

(1979)

My house

My mother lives in a house
where nobody has ever died

she surrounds herself
and her family with light

each time I go home
I feel she is washing
and ironing the clothes of death

these clothes for work
and for going out
to the Club on Sunday
and for Jenny to take her baby
to the doctor in

death comes on the television
and mum laughs

saying there's death again
I must get those jeans taken up

My granny

When my granny was dying
I'd go into her bedroom
and look at her

she'd tell me to get out of it
leave this foul river

it will wear you out too

she was very sick
and her red curly hair
was matted and smelt of gin

sometimes I sat there all day
listening to the races
and put bets on for her at the shop

and I sat there the afternoon
she died and heard her say her last words
I sat there not telling

maybe three hours
beside the first dead person I'd seen

I tried to drink some of her gin
it made me throw up on the bed
then I left her

she said the prawns will eat you
when you die on the Hawkesbury River

The harbour bridge

I went with dad on the sulky
into town across the harbour bridge

it was a windy cold day

I wasn't too keen on going
along in a horse and cart in the city

I slid down under the seat
so the horse's tail swished in my face

we passed trams and women
standing at the crossings

and dad just driving through it all
as if he was still up the river

his hat on his head
and his son beside him
with the city grit getting on me

the shopping growing in the back
beans and tomato trees

the blood and bone spilling behind us

My first proper girlfriend

The first girl I wanted to marry
was Joan Hunter
her father owned more oyster leases
than anyone else on the river

she had buck teeth
but she looked okay really

we'd sit on her father's wharf
and watch the mullet together for hours

they will take over the world one day

we loved each other all right

my parents hated us being together
and called her Bugs Bunny

One night my father cut Joan's dad
with a fishing knife
right down his left cheek

that little protestant bludger
with his stuck-up bitch of a daughter

My tenth birthday

We went to Pumpkin Point
for my tenth birthday

the best picnic beach on the river

the mud is thinner
and doesn't smell as off

and there is a swing
made from a huge truck tyre

I wore my first jeans
and got a cane rod and a bird book

Dad washed the rabbit blood
out of the back of his truck
and we spread grey blankets
and pillows over the splinters

A storm came up after lunch
and I cut my foot open
on a sardine can as I ran into a cave

it was the same cave
I found again four years later
on a night my father set out the nets

and slept beside me
for the only time in his life

My fishing boat

Mum and dad are at it again
in the room
next to mine
their terrible sobbing
comes through the damp wall

they fight about something
I have done

I get out of bed
and go down the yard to the river
push my boat out into
the black and freezing bay

under the mangroves
that smell like human shit

I move along my secret channel
my hands blistered
from rowing slip with blood
around the cove I tie up on a mangrove
it rains harder

all I catch are catfish here
and have them sliding
about in the belly of the boat

they are the ugliest-looking things
in the world

Growing up alone

1

Walking down our backyard
scraping my legs on blackberries

at the steps I pull on the ropes
holding up the old twine
gill-net used for
trapping starlings now

they hit it
then flap out
until they strangle themselves
the same as mullet

I tear out the birds at eye level
ripping the weak mesh
and throw the bodies onto the compost

its heap spreading down
to the tide-line
putrescence curling out
from the warm centre where blowflies

cluster in the thick of it

2

Me and Sandy would go
out onto the mudflats at low tide
catching soldier crabs

we'd talk about what would happen
if she ever got pregnant to me

because we were first cousins
our baby would have
one of those big heads

and maybe no hand or something

3

Sandy was pretty ugly too

blotched freckles on her screwed-up face
skinny legs and no tits

good hair though
curly and real yellow

she always had cold sores on her lips
that tasted salty

4

At midday I'd walk to the Point
and there'd be nobody

I'd look at the starlings
the only things that could take it
hard birds that shine

eating anything just about
one day I watched them get through a cat
that'd been run over

it took them a morning

5

Sandy knew a place at Cheero Point
where we'd go behind a tree
and stare into the eyes of God

they were in the face
of an old yellow cat who'd gone mad

once we looked we wouldn't be able to move
sitting there for hours sometimes
before it let us go

6

The backyard to our grandfather's
was the Hawkesbury River

and me and Sandy hated it
It meant all the kids at Gosford
knew how poor we were

because only fishermen lived there
and we hated it because

when you went out on it at night
the dark was frightening
and the ground was full of ants

the river with its savage tides
that would wear you out in half an hour

and in summer the heat
and sun burning into your neck

giving you awful headaches
and nothing to do but fish or hide

7

I'd been crying under the house

I ran out onto the road
into the same dust and heat again

with the lousy starlings
the dark sheen on their wings
oily metallic green

I thought about the way we die

the steps just falling away
from under me as I ran

the heads of jewfish
nailed out along the wharf rail

two hundred and seven
some skulls and others still flesh

all with their eyes eaten out

8

In town I had this game it was all different
that the papershop wasn't neat
and the pub didn't smell so rotten

I'd sit in dad's truck and look out
at the town's light
a clear steady light
nothing like the river's

softer and shifting
and with people walking through it

9

Along the shore in the mud
I'd walk all day alone

and wonder how come nothing
ever happened to me

how come I didn't go mad or something

mud caked all over me
and my face throbbing with sun

and never seeing anyone

10

We cover our faces with mud
and become hunters
in the mangroves barefoot and nude
our arms sting from cuts

we talk less until we only make sounds

Sandy gets the first bird
an old wood duck
we share its feathers on the run

then onto the mudflats
our feet sinking in four feet of mud
where the big crabs swim

out here branches rot away
and we pull each other
up out of the mud by our hair

soon you don't feel things
and you have to get back to the rocks

before you realise what you've
been doing all day

CODA

Fishing skiff in the light
at Mackerel Flats, mud-caked, sun borne
by the old man caulking cracks.

Rust scales drop from boat-slip
to silt as he moves.

Gnawed, hacked heads of black bream
rock through the wash.

Skeleton trophies, Banjo Rays,
staked out on a pile,
their whip tails paralyzed chalk.

Light seeps through the folds of his turkey neck –
his eyes don't blink

and flick out involuntarily to where
mud-gudgers pick at the heads.

He is alone with his tinkering work.
He holds the scraper
like a little axe and chips
away at the belly of his boat.

My afternoon

I think of sex all afternoon

it becomes memory
the wide beds
and the fleshy women

who got me here

the mornings are best
spent alone
I can't do anything in the mornings
with women any more

I am taken from place to place
as I pretend
to be good about sex

then quite drunk
I lie back in the folds
of their particular sheets

face buried in fear near shame

from

THE LAW AT HEART'S DESIRE
(1982)

Rimbaud having a bath

To have been held down in a park
the animal breath on your face
hands tightening on the throat
grappling at you in the dark
a life lashing out to embrace
the flesh and green bones under it
and then the infected slime
injected by the half-erect cock

Remains a flesh wound until
morning and poetry begin their work
in the carnage under the skull

The great poet goes home again
to his mother and becomes
the boy he is and feels the pain
subside his senses numbed
by the fire boiling the water
and the yellow soap in the copper

He takes a rag and pumice stone
and slides his naked body in

Because he has taken this bath
he has betrayed his art
having washed the vermin
from the body and the heart

The home, the spare room

I am the poet of the spare room
the man who lives here

with television's
incessant coloured noise

between the ads keeping the children
at bay

At night I walk the seagrass
down the hall

my head rolls before me
like some kind of a round dice

which room tonight?

I think of my wife-to-be
who has thrown herself down

in a foetal shape onto her bed

I am a hard man, a vicious seer
who simply wants

to go on living – love is beyond me

if it exists – my heart,
so called, is as efficient as a bull's

and as desperate
for the earth's treasures –

I turn into the spare room
and begin to write a poem of infinite

tenderness

Into forest

My face the long grey fish drifts above
the soft floor over the leaves
returning to their previous lives

it looks into the centre of spores
clustered under the tree fern fronds with eyes
trying to forget

High above where I have never lived

a thornbill jets through the twigs
and the rufus whistlers begin their territorial
alarms – So I am finally here

watching my face searching for the next mask

In the house my wife is moving behind
sheets of glass holding the pages of sleep
I can't read – she awaits

the time we have been trying for
the moments without wings we can never own
she looks out at my face

It is a life I am unable to recall or imagine

In the house among the spotted gums
my face has been up all night talking to itself
speaking in tongues

crashing about in the living room
a bowerbird caged-in growing weak

in panic howling

Here in the bush it makes no sound
the eyes join the moving sky
and the mouth draws in more air for its lies

the black tongue a broken wing
and the beaked nose a dorsal before the chin's bristle

I try to remember a face in a language
we speak trees in

In the night

The sheets are wrapped about me
I wake in a bad mood
you stand in the centre of it
It's been four days since I was with you
now you enter my dreams
in the same mood as I left you
petulant your head in
some old tantrum
I untangle myself and get up
then walk out into the dark house
my feet pad the cold
once again I hear the empty words
repeating promises vows a pledge
impossible charms against old age and despair
We have all our lives left to live through
why must watch ourselves
here in the present repeating our
selves our love hopeless
we hack away at our heads
our faces tense rubbing in the salt
our skin drawn the top lips
hanging loose
We have made the rendezvous
though each time we meet and touch
is another wound that will not heal
Why do we insist on being
real this way there is
a life each day the colours
surround us and at night we work
or sleep between television
and the bright moments of solitude
strange dreams of courage
I reach the kitchen moonlight
the smell of cooked meat
the luminous circle of the stove-clock
I turn and go back into
the living room
my family is sleeping I sit at my desk
and stare at the blue machine
In your house across the harbour
you wake turn on your side and curse me
Okay call me a ghost of a man

Glass Bay sonnets

I wanted you to know all about my new life
wondered what you would think of it
waiting here at the gates of hell
the stove burning the breakfast toast
another morning scraping away
in the hedge-lined garden where the petals
of the black-eyed susan have fallen
like orange moths along the path

I wanted you to see for yourself what you
were not missing out on these days
though I knew you would be thinking of me
cool underneath the peppermint tree
looking out across the bay at the seagulls
raking the tide for whitebait

Well yes my kitchen window does look over
Glass Bay and the parrots chatter
through the bushy trees their sheen of
flashy colour bright in the green foliage
at night the flying foxes climb in the figs
the darkness is so calm I sleep again
I have discovered the secrets
of description by simply living here

Only yesterday three great black cockatoos
came swooping into our garden
we gave them bread and nuts to eat
their screeching terrified the cat so much
she sprang up onto the terrace
a frenzied ball of fur in the potted geraniums

I climbed to calm her and she hissed and spat
and clawed my arm across a vein
and though I pulled back quickly there was
blood in the kitchen and a teatowel streaked
trails splattering across the floor
the severed vein gushing into the sink
swirling with tap water and stale tea-leaves
I was so astonished I felt no pain

I know it's nothing to write home about
though I try sitting here surrounded by a view
where the bay ebbs and the gulls squabble
in the wash for the dead and injured bait
and a yacht its sail a membrane that trembles
with light pulls out from the marina

Landscape

The grey wharf creaks under my weight
maybe a hundred years
since these piles were driven in
and the planks laid across
The river moves slowly over mudbanks
swallows dive and glide through clouds
of white ants in the low sky
I take my fishing rod in my hands
shift weight onto one leg
and cast the bait in a long and graceful arc
It splashes beside an old snag
I look across the river at a derelict house
its for-sale sign askew
on the paling fence and the garden
a bush of rusted wire in the yard the great
hulk of a wrecked Chevrolet

from

THE CLEAN DARK
(1989)

Remembering posts

(for Manfred Jurgensen)

In this country, beyond the sparkle
and the junk, the weekend blood
arenas, beaches full of paddlepops
and shit, out along the road
you stop noticing flags for hamburgers
or the empire, it all becomes a streak
of colour smearing the windscreen –
as you drift freeways or swerve
and loop down narrow passes you
realise you could be anywhere
in the world in your head, though
nowhere else you'd feel like this –
a passenger of memory – floating out
across centuries. After distance
lulls you become a mobile antenna,
taking it in as each nerve flicks
with pain, sensing flesh wounds
in the open-cut mountainside, broken
bones under desert crust. Now you
know that if you stop you would shoot
roots and grow branches, leaves,
flowers – or you'd spear yourself
into the earth and sprout up
like a telegraph pole, a grey post
on the edge of a gibber plain, and be
stuck there swaying in the dry wind,
remembering.

Green prawn map

(in memory of my grandfather H.T. Adamson)

Morning before sunrise, sheets of dark air
   hang from nowhere in the sky.
No stars there, only here is river.

   His line threads through a berley trail,
a thread his life. There's no wind
   in the world and darkness is a smell alive

   with itself. He flicks
a torch, a paper map *Hawkesbury River*
   & District damp, opened out. No sound
but a black chuckle

   as fingers turn the limp page.
Memory tracks its fragments, its thousand winds,
   shoals and creeks, collapsed shacks

a white gap, mudflats – web over web
   lace-ball in brain's meridian.
This paper's no map, what are its lines

   as flashlight conjures a code
from a page of light, a spider's a total blank?
   So he steers upstream now

away from map-reason, no direction to take
   but hands and boat to the place
where he will kill prawns, mesh and scoop

   in creek and bay and take
his bait kicking green out from this translucent
   morning.

   Flint & Steel shines
behind him, light comes in from everywhere,
   prawns are peeled alive.

Set rods, tips curve along tide, the prawns howl
   into the breeze, marking the page.
He works alone to do this kind of work –

   his face hardened in sun, hands
moving in and out of water and his life.

The channels
(for Orlando)

At Mooney there had been killing
from the start, from mudflat to creek –

in the name of the river spirits,
it was death to the fish: so the shores

are hallowed where we fought for your future
through silence on deep water.

Fierce heads breaking ancient tide
and I called blood, feathers and scale,

my boy, bones of the trees –
I had forgotten love until you

stood your ground, though it was a child's

and filled with the new laws of cities.
I was afraid for your senses

and soul; so here I'll twist phrases
to sing again the old lores

and say the love a father would –
there with your eyes filled with the shiny

life, your dreams of style, jets
and tropical adventures, you were a savage

pride with a high mind aflame.
I shook as I spoke you down, rocked

to the bone by your blunt tongue –
and I will again engage your temper

with the magic of language:
let me offer what I can as a hard man

softened by my becoming a father
to you, of your unknowable

future, questing and burning for more now,
that we go on always.

Songs for Juno

I

My lies are for you, take them utterly, along
with the truth we are explorers for.
An old skiff mutters, pushes up Hawkesbury mud –
the image comes in, drifts, sinks, disappears:
shape-changing gods, we dream in separate bodies;
a part of it, we want feathers for sails;
the rivers we are dancing stand upright in the sky,
distance between them – though at headlands
fork, touching mix, become ocean.

II

Wind and the sails full in dreaming with you.
We talk of great deserts, old chalk cities,
ice language and its lava. Then imagination darts,
Tasmania appears filling our bedroom, sails
are wings of geese, homing ocean, white tricks
of the distance. How do we depart our tiny pasts?
My love, time fragments, blows into space –
we ride, fly, sail in every way we find there is
to now. Bring us a new language, to remake
these questions, into dream, the gale, I whisper
to you softly.

III

How long in these secret places from childhood –
the old embers smoulder on, the lowlands
laced with fire-lines, long spokes turning
in sky – were we at play – or were the games more
half-remembered charms, songs? We inhabit,
are rocked by still those innocent passions.
Dressed up for the new ritual, we move
the circle more than dance it. Take the moment,
hold it to you, the new, my brave and frightened
lover is a sacramental kiss. Our dreams touch –
warm with light. Give me your nightmares too.

IV

Paint flaking from the belly of an old clinker.
The boys with their rods, prawns
and bloodworms rubbed through their hair,
tasting the westerly around Snake Island –
and you sleeping, curled around the stern.
The mountains everywhere, skirts of the mangroves,
then at Dangar's jetty, an octopus
sucking for its life at the end of a line.
Blue wrens hovering for invisible insects, a shag
hunched on a wing. The trim park
patched there amongst the scribbly gums,
houses, a wash-shed, and in a backyard
lemongrass drying in the sunlight.

V

The new list begins.

American sonnet

(for John Forbes)

I am the snow bandit who must travel
in the red dirt night, this hat is
for style more than anything, shade
amuses me, or the idea of shade
I should say as no such thing exists
in the spirit world of talk. I wrestle
butterflies of light with my gaze,
these strange tracks that I leave
are for the anthropologist of morning;
ash fills my pockets as I fold away
sheets of anything resembling thought;
all I go by is the way it feels, no
thing bothers me unless it hurts.
I don't know what worship is for, let
alone what it is – I tried once in
swampland to the north of here to
describe talk, but no such luck, no
such pain, yes even words perish
from lack of care, lack of use.

The Jesus bird

The lotus-bird's signature
is slenderness, moving
without ring-marking water's
skin-tight surface.
A colourist, strokes tone
with a wing, fans out pinions:
His show's to escape
death in shape of harrier
or swamp's light-slashing pike.
The night watch is a dance
where bird antenna
probes mind-stepping illusion
to parry with
a stray plug-throwing fisherman,
alert in thin air
whirred by dragonfly's
cellophane propeller
puttering fat swamp-bug.
When the creek's back is dark
glass, a conjurer – striper, lotus
dancing with river-pimps –
it's creek alley's side-show.

Fishing with my stepson

We wake by your watch on my wrist,
its piercing silicon chip
alarm bat-squealing, needling
through our room in the Angler's Rest.
We drink Coke from a plastic Esky
with ice melting into newspaper-
wrapped squid, the only
unfrozen bait in town. In perfect dawn
we set out from *Don's Boats*,
the outboard ploughs us through a bay,
at Juno Point we cast our silver
Tobys, our new Swedish lures.
Your pure graphite rod flashes
at first light – a graceful cast
sails out fine as a spiderweb,
the smooth water mirrors the arc.
A year passes in the minute it takes
for you to reel in your first true catch,
the rod-bending, line-singing
realising strike and the flash of fish-fire,
the final buck underwater dash
of a school jewfish, its explosion in air,
and for that split second of communion
between us, utter wonder.

Couplets

(for Juno)

On days still when the tide's full, river
hours with you are momentary fire

in the head, shall not stay memories
even, so intensely lived: just to sense

bay calm and watch the seconds scatter.
These cupped hands of brackish water

evaporate as light fragments in hair flicker
with mangrove's shade for your skin —

I know grassbanks where we rolled together
on the shaggy cotton-brush, now remember

not to remember any day other than our morning
on Jerusalem Bay, there as tide turned

the stern, our boat was afloat on a mist
rolling in, full of the song of the wattlebird.

Silva

It came into being from the splintered limbs
swam out and flowered into being

from chopped saplings and wood-chips
its pages glowing and telling their numbers

this a numbat's fragile skeleton
this the imprint of the last chalk-moth

Members of court in the old languages
mumbled as wings of ground parrots flicked

at night we discovered new seeds
in an old gum's stump as shoals of insect memory

floated out from a bee-eater's nest
then the rasping call of an adder

We looked into the white-rimmed eyes of the elders
and wanted to turn away

until pages began stroking air
that carried back doves from the black bamboo

Australia the goshawk circled a lake
we croaked amphibian prayers to reflected skies

then stumbled off through the spinifex

Mornings threaded the whale bones with flame
as poetry baked like a rock

on the final page of dense black marble
of slate-thought that shone

until the eyes of a hunstman took us
into morning's spokes a white trap-work

where caught finches hung their hearts drumming

Australia we sobbed through the paperbarks' songs
to birds and the gentle animals

and to the soft-stepping people of its river-banks

Clear water reckoning

I write into the long black morning,
out here on the end of the point,
far from my wife in Budapest –
as the river cuts through a mountain
in Sydney a poet is launching
his new volume *Under Berlin*
and I feel like Catullus on Rome's edge
but this passes and I turn to face
the oncoming dawn, the house
breathes tidal air as the night
fires outside with barking owls,
marsupials rustling, the prawn bird
beginning its taunting dawn whistle;
I burn the electricity
and measure hours by the lines –
I have strewn words around the living room,
taken them out from their
sentences, left them unused wherever
they fell; they are the bait –
I hunch over my desk and start to row,
let the tide flow in, watch
the window, with the door locked now
I wait – hear satin bowerbirds
scratching out the seeds from bottlebrush.
Dawn is a thin slit of illuminated
bowerbird blue along mountain lines,
in this year of cock and bull
celebration the TV goes on unwatched
upstairs, I hear it congratulating us
for making Australia what it is –
the heater breathes out a steady stream
of heated air – I go deeper
into my head, I see the Hawkesbury
flowing through Budapest, the Hungarians
do not seem to mind, they are bemused,
the river parts around their spires and domes,
I see other cities, whole cultures
drawn from territories within,
though with this freedom
comes a feeling of strange panic
for the real; so I get on
with it, writing out from this egg
holding my thought in a turbulent knot,

a bunched-up octopus. I steer
away from anything confessional,
thinking of Robert Lowell crafting
lines of intelligent blues,
his Jelly Roll of a self-caught mess
deep in spiritual distress.
Outside the river pulls me back,
shafts of light disintegrate into clues,
flecked symbols shine with order –
the bowerbirds have woven colour
around the house, through
bushes blue patterns of themselves
traced about the place; half
the moon can topple a mountain,
anything is possible here
I remind myself and begin to hum,
flattening out all the words that were
impossible to write today. I hum
out all the poems I should have
written, I hum away now also
the desire to write from memory –
there is enough sorrow in the present.
I look out over the incoming tide, dark racks
of oysters jut from its ink.

The details necessary

Tar on the dirt drifts to afternoon's
edges, slopes of winter, animals
and birds in the ground, trees –
the domed sky's early stars strung
to earth by tails of mist.
The full moon is translucent orange
and moves the far mountain
deeper into distance. I know words
will trouble my poem tonight
though I can't be bothered
with all that, anyway I'm sure
Susan Sontag is working on it,
somewhere in Greece or maybe
New York, sitting at her wicker table
facing some wall or window
full of intricate geometries –
or maybe she's given up reading books
again and just sits there,
her head rocking with the puzzle
of Artaud's Platonic imagery, who
knows – though she's sure
to be covering the problems of things
like this: writing poetry in '88
on the side of a river in Australia;
she'll be thinking about
the 'old questions', dovetailing
them into the new. Tonight
I'll open my lines to love, desire –
desire for my wife, craving for a chance
to love her here, under
orange Hawkesbury moon, taking her
into our bedroom, turning out
the electricity, opening the window,
holding her until we shine with carnality,
dropping awhile the weight of poetry, art,
photography – though maybe using
them for loving until our bones are
liquid fire – our bodies given
to each other in postures
of alchemy and praise, as if we
were the gods we have relentlessly
tried to believe through others.

Here we would be new and know it as we
fondled our imaginations
through our bodies; I would take her
carefully and begin to kiss
from her toes slowly up into the little
wings of her cunt, her breasts
until her long nipples were full
in my mouth; our hands following
our hearts until our bodies arched over
the bed in colours our senses
would invent for the rest of our lives,
and live then the hours
in all the details that are necessary,
as complex as the language
Susan Sontag needs to use when
she shares with us her passion
and admiration for Artaud's mystic poems,
where flesh and thought are one,
where the day becomes the poem looking into
what must be done.

Sonnets for Robert Duncan

1

Life today is a flowering bush of blue,
the windy harbour's alive with light,
red sun turns city glass to sheets of silk.
It's afternoon, the reflections caught

by translucent bays marble edges of the view –
bitter news is distilled by polite talk,
death has arrived again, hearing of it
shears from memory images of Francis Webb,

another poet who sang words into thought,
made phrases abstract for a figurative God.
Now Duncan's death succeeds more

than most, his life opened days, brought
song to nights where silence riddled prayer.
It isn't enough to weave more silk

2

the rhetoric's a holy gibberish, and cocoons
have fallen to their hungry worms
before they're even spun: I have only
a dumb reaper and Duncan's hand-woven psalms,

only the poetry. Only his words
and for all his talk of angels, they become
also creatures of the language we spoke in.
I imagine his consternation with 'only'

Only the poem! I hear the strict tone
in reprimand, music of anger composing itself,
though now impossibly. Here I point

to his death, still even surrounded by it --
pouring from heaven or rising from the stench,
only the poem, though be compelled begin another.

3

Make this death's loom, take up the lyre
strung to play rhymes pulled taut across
slangy syntax, something of calm awareness
in song, a finality grows from loss –

What does the Worm work in its cocoon?
Do I finally understand this arcane question?
revealing the silken vanity of talk
with death – though why reprimand a tone

of voice when it's the content
breaking the news – as now the red sun
is being eaten on a glass building-side

by a flashing neon sign spelling out
black homilies and jingles for the State:
have safe sex and spoil the Reaper's fun.

4

Now shred all irony to ribbons and trail
them from a ferry leaving Kirribilli wharf
in memory of Frank Webb – he sailed
there with his grandfather and walked

by the coal freighters where he'd meditate –
he called himself a pirate of peace
as he traced with his fingers a carved shark
that sanctified the rock. It is a place

poets have sung for centuries, so I take
a bearing here for Duncan, amidst languages
that shape this bay into a face –

though whose? Whoever's god now assuages
the harbourside with songs we can belong to,
life-torn words for death's menagerie.

No river, no death

1

Awake after years: sudden exploding mangroves
alight as Mooney vanishes in mountain shade –

late afternoon, confusion of words, language
alive with a life of its own, lashing

out then licking its flesh wounds.
Words of the river, swarming in branches

of mangrove with prawn birds and fruit bats
and mullet butting upstream,

schooling, leaping,
and bull-nosed singing mullet songs –

silver green needs being spun till the spawn is done.

The river hawks tear at the heart's flesh, eat,
love to fly, in a moment's pocket of heaved air

where they are mullet's fear. Though here
on the tide's line, a torn wing of stingray

waves in wash, prawns fester on the underside.

2

Now leave from a jetty, souls going where souls go.
The world's a mudbank in a dank westerly

and there's nothing to hand, nothing to hold,
death's all around in the afternoon air.

Here with the spirits of river gods, the lost,
lost in a holy place, its histories

entangled with sadness, deep sorrow's
in the rotting and remembering.

Over this: planks, cut from swamp, return –
hewn from trunks in their green years

now creaking complainers in the dull sun.

The wharf sags with tar-drenched oyster racks
and a fisherman's punt rocks at its side for Charon.

3

Nets circle the mullet school, the fishermen
shake their mesh and the old rope stings

the stumped fingers and crooked thumbs,
then the fish buck under and die

in the net's wing-lock; like a cloak cast
out from the fishers' minds the green tide's

gone black and the mullet are done,
hauled to their death from the spawning run.

4

Now here in a creek on Mooney Bay all river
life calms the head that broods

on politicians oceans away, microwaved
down to our side of the planet,

their sickness infecting the silt of this tide.
They are death men rattling loaded dice,

war-headed malformations of the mind
as an eyeless reaper, its cloak space-fabric,

its titanium blade, its skull powdering radium,
with the crippling power of crab-thought

turning its claws onto its own black flesh.

To feel it here with the ancient river
alive in a crawling

flying prehistoric line drawn on a rock –
here in the belly of the serpent's beginnings –

is to know we may not go where all souls go.

5

We live with the threat of that white flash
until again like hawks we gamble

with flesh, with oblivion – talons of the soul
along the heart in memory's flood –

and tear from the thin blue wind the black heart
of the cave our sick heads come from.

6

The afternoon's last light has gone under now.
A flying fox swims in through a star,

catfish are pecking the stingray's wing.
The larrikin prawn bird starts to sing.

Farming the oysters

They move their black stick bundles
across the river, put stakes
aside for fresh water, making racks
to drench in tar; oyster-farmers
who strive for an order
of their own, gardening their shells
bunching up smoked mullet
assorting old bleached branches
along a ragged shore –
on the stern-end of their punts
they stand. Staring straight ahead,
solitary figures, they power
along, driven by 100-horse Mercs
burning up and down the river,
blind drunk through dangerous
light; they bore towards shacks
tucked in the upper reaches,
proud-looking gentlemen in black
contemplating the stern's metal music.

What's slaughtered's gone

How long then since
that night in the creek
when you killed
the creek? Can it be
long now, it's calm
again here, though
I don't mean in the head,
here on the rock
where you sat smoking
wet fags, yes this same
rock, it remembers
not a fish left living
and you laughing.
How long since you made
your mark, eh, as you
shivered mad in blood –
though not calm
in the head then, it was
wrecking-night swamp
and it was happy
you were on that rock
drenched and yelling.
Nets strung through
the paperbarks to dry –
then a crow caught up.
Now think of that black
flapping yellow eye
looking when you took
Mandy back there
in a fisherman's shack,
deserted and windowless
with that black-rag-bird
in with her voice there
with a flapping wing
tangled in hair and you
outside on a rock
smoking with the mullet
in a heap and rotting –
for how long was
she there with you
out of your head
with the pitch of her
screaming. And so

did you look down as her
and see as feathers
danced on the dirt floor
dark leaves of plants
from the swamp were
your wraps to bundle
and pack the stinking fish
then dump them as love
at the door of the shack.
As her as the sun
came up did you see
honeyeaters rolling out
from flowering gums
and with her hands feel
cuts from cracked oystershell,
with your toes in thick
mud of the gully, who
shook branches as wattle
showered down on it all
till a crow flicked
through a tree, on a rock
by the shack up there
on that calm salt creek.

Wild colonial boys

Musk ducks and the plump Wonga pigeon
were knocked from the sky
in blood sport, left to rot, then afterwards
in firelight were the games,
all various forms of gambling. In the mist
you'd hear knuckle-bones rattle
in their cotton pockets or, darned
in conversation, obscene words, slurred
by badly brewed alcohol; never song
but garbled recitations, coughed half-chants.
Whatever fed the imagination
was like a yellowness: it showed
in various activities, from plucking
ducks to the way they slept in postures
of loose decadence. The river
was a flood of their refuse, a smear of thick
waste through the countryside. After
storms and at low tide you'd see the details
of their hate: the score, a tally and what they called
their stake – the sacred remnants
of an ancient tribe's estate.

Canticle for the bicentennial dead

They are talking, in their cedar-benched rooms
on French-polished chairs, and they talk

in reasonable tones, in the great stone buildings
they are talking firmly, in the half-light

and they mention at times the drinking of alcohol,
the sweet blood-coloured wine the young drink,

the beer they share in the riverless river-beds
and the backstreets, and in the main street –

in government-coloured parks, drinking
the sweet blood in recreation patches, campsites.

They talk, the clean-handed ones, as they gather
strange facts; and as they talk

collecting words, they sweat under nylon wigs.
Men in blue uniforms are finding the bodies,

the uniforms are finding the dead: young hunters
who have lost their hunting, singers who

would sing of fish are now found hung –
crumpled in night-rags in the public's corners;

discovered there broken, lit by stripes
of regulated sunlight beneath the whispering

rolling cell window bars. Their bodies
found in postures of human-shaped effigies,

hunched in the dank sour urinated atmosphere
near the bed-board, beside cracked lavatory bowls,

slumped on the thousand grooved, fingernailed walls
of your local police station's cell –

bodies of the street's larrikin koories
suspended above concrete in the phenyl-thick air.

Meanwhile outside, the count continues: on radio,
on TV, the news – like Vietnam again, the faces

of mothers torn across the screens –
and the poets write no elegies, our artists

cannot describe their grief, though
the clean-handed ones paginate dossiers

and court reporters' hands move over the papers.

from

WARDS OF THE STATE

(1990)

Social realist

There's no one in charge here
though I do the talking, there are
some things you could put into words
just in case, not that you'd use them.
This is no flash racecourse where
punks have resumés – sure, I might
get out of it, but just give me the nod
and I'll speak with grating accuracy
just to be a nuisance. These
impossible words exist in a desert
called lifestyle: write and they
call you Headspace. Up the road
there's a movie on, directed
by some fashionable bent German –
it shows how gullible imaginations
fall for the 'look' of an evil
designer. This destructive
nymph splashed black across the
screen's been pasteurised, but gets
them in: today she's head-down in
astro-turf, blown out
posing for a B-grade porno
and who know's what city she
thinks she's in, head shaved,
beyond time, squinting through
the new conjunctivitis.

Sign this

I'll sign anything, in case you hadn't
noticed: my name means nothing
really, no bank takes it seriously
and shops call for the police
at the sound of it; the police see it
written on reports and throw them
into the shredders; my son rubs it
from the envelope he uses
to carry his favourite photographs in;
my name is shit I won't plague
you with the details – I can't give it away
and it follows me through hell – when
the bell tolls for me, it'll be an imposter
they put on my grave.

State ward sonnet

The mess hall by shimmering glass reflected
in porridge bowls' brown sugar-flavoured

winter gets under the nails of a boy
who'll darn his socks on his hand machine

His behaviour's a new art to annoy
and he'll pat dry yellow blisters between

his fingers with a cloth tucked into his sleeve
Daydreams get buried weeding the beans

So bring back the marching songs
They've got to be better than a hole in solitude

He rocks back on his raw haunches for long
enough to weave more letters in his head

Mother comes out spelling 'other' tattooed in
five separate letters on each finger in red

Kenneth Slessor dancing

Whenever he looked through windows,
in life or poetry, he'd wake that other self
inside ourselves, then send it dancing
    out – the man who isn't me

he'd say, there's the true dancing dandy,
sliding those Italian two-tones lightly
over an evening's whistling floor,
    just twirling elegance.

He'd go dropping the pretensions even more
in light of the imagined nights
of a devil laid bare who might be there –
    old ghost, the cock,

who cares? The words fell from his dance;
his toes would never be hurting, he'd toss off
the formality of shoes and shed his skin
    like a garter snake –

and skinless, over the periwinkles, rocks,
dancing in lapping tides, no shoes or socks,
he'd laugh at the Grey Nurse in the surf
    perfecting a jig or two.

Then back in his flat on Billyard Avenue
he'd watch the harbour and along the shores
improbable plausibilities would renew
    his wobbling libido.

Gazing through his window one morning he saw
the milkman. Ken listened to him chink
chinking bottles, put his finger to the glass,
    tried to rethink

his choreography – jerked back with a pang –
in pain his hand crabbed open, to pass
through glass – a dancer's circle – back
    to end song as it began.

Boat with an empty mind

1

Nine cats float their eyes above the shore;
each pair of globes, lit from within,
scatters as I move suddenly and kick over
     an outboard motor.

Magenta's feathery clouds uncurl the sky.
This is no boat: a roaring head of metal
growls and spits as I toil with a rope
     coiled in slimy loops.

I slip it into the belly and stand back –
call you high in the light, beckoning
with my hands, darling I say, quick look
     it's all gone black.

The surface mirrors dark as a cat takes
a flying leap to the white pylon,
misses and smacks into the river's flow –
     it flies up the totem,

exploding with salt. We end up alone
again; a crew of two, we rumble over
the low-lying mudflats, gaze into our
     prehistoric mountain,

its windows ablaze with light.
You paint strange figures with your eyes.
We splash through a jet-black tide,
     watch freeways climb

in concrete scrolls into mountains.
The outboard motor coughs, we slough in mud.
Out from Coleridgean darkness a lifeboat
     empty by our side.

2

We kiss and it turns to winter. Our kiss
will be a site for others, collecting stars
that shoot by; lovers will gather, some
    beckoning to promise.

We follow through, trailing trinkets, lures –
artefacts to sculpt and charm our souls –
back from this vast black mirror-speckled dark
    stars in parchment

and rock face: remember the steady elders
making this crossing, in dugouts sewn
with wattle bark? They notice kissing lovers;
    chuckling, they know.

Ode on Beckett's death

Take back the day though there's no
one to say that to

for I would give the day away
& let someone else spell out

words for the deal
& who's making it

no one can say
cleave these syllables

through the knot my tongue is
torn against the devil

who does not have to spell out
words bunged into words

grief yes give us grief for god's sake

from

WAVING TO HART CRANE

(1994)

Rock carving with Kevin Gilbert

The fish outlined on the rock
is the shape of a mulloway, we are moving
here under a fine yellow rain
pouring from the spear wound
in its side. A lyrebird dances above,
trembling the morning silk air.
We fish with two swamp harriers,
sweet whistling killers like us, who cut
fish throats and clasp up
bunches of silver nerves –
calling under stars convicts
hacked in the cliff face.
We crush oysters with rocks
and throw them as berley into the tide
we call our Milky Way.
After a while stingrays
come on the bite, then one after
another, brown-winged,
hump-backed, yellow-bellied
bull-rays fight to their death –
we cut some free to watch slide
over carvings of themselves,
back into the drink, as the rock mulloway
moves its shallowing grooves.

Folk song

(for Kevin Hart)

We live here by this
sliding water, brown by day
black at night

flecked with bats
and the blue powdery stars.
Morning, a kingfisher

sits, an indigo rock
knife-shaped, winking
sun-speckled. There are too

many of us here,
still they keep coming,
rockets and landmines pock

their dreams. Here
the long-billed ibis go savage
in the mangroves:

Egyptians, blown in
on some cosmic whim, they
plunge their heads

into the black mud swamp
and drag out long bloodworms;
the royal spoonbills

shake their crowns,
head feathers white calligraphy
of surrender. We sing

of the mulloway, our
mauve-scaled river cod. They
rise breaking the surface,

our songs mention
mulloway kills and at night
we eat the rich cream-coloured flesh.

Waving to Hart Crane

Farewell to the wire,
the voices on
the line. Goodbye
switchboard rider, my

American friend.
We enter the new
century through glass,
black oceans

and black winds,
thin fibre funnelling
poetry out
of existence.

No sonnet will survive
the fax on fire,
out-sound that hash
of voices slung up

from the cable.
Tip your hat
and flicker with
smoke from silent movies,

there are no more
cunning gaps left
on the cutting room
floor by editors.

Here they expunge
the message, nothing's
praise. If gestures
appear they fold in fade-out.

Cornflowers

(in memoriam Robert Harris)

In a skiff, anchored
on the edge of a mangrove
swamp, he gave me

a version,
an unpolished song,
something that might have

gone unspoken
in our bright lives;
there is no dark side

he told me: things
will glow, sing or die though
if we want them to,

it's all alive,
I just want to know who
owns the conversation

we may have some day, who
owns the dialogue
he repeated as

a flathead slapped
and shuddered
in the belly of the boat,

its pale speckles
flaring, the blue
barred tail fanning air,

who owns the words
as they hovered
with plump mosquitoes

and collided with
a whiting in flight
down a cadence of dancing

particles, our
hearts locked in their
cages of singing muscle;

it was concerning
this theme, he continued,
that I composed a tune

for the cornflowers
to sing, cut, sitting
on my table in an indigo jar.

The Australian crawl

I watched your body fluttering across
the pool, your hands little buckets
chucking water on the flames. The bushfire
was background music as the kids

sploshed about in the wading area –
all this time and we believed our bodies
meant something, life at least.
Birthdays shivered up our spines,

sparks in the pallid undergrowth of hair
greying and uncurling. In this dream
our first picnic sails along
on a blanket just above the flames,

the women wearing gingham frocks
making it seem so very sad, Uncle John
juggling his belly on a tricycle,
the bacon-rind on the sliced bread

a wizened hieroglyph meaning nothing,
the cucumber circles sitting on the sockets
of your mother's eyes. Back at home
on the shelf conch-shells

sitting next to books become
little inkwells of nasty belief,
the silver we never used dancing
on the table like soft silver tadpoles –

sequential meanings drift into meltdown.
The pale-headed rosella's a smudge
on the bathroom mirror, the whole house
is full of an awful music chuffing

and percussing in your head –
a rat-a-tat and an Australian threadfin
salmon comes down south while you're
fishing hookless in the sky.

A picture becomes three-dimensional: it's
Tassie the cat, fleas scooting down his tail
into the fish-tank. Outside cockatoos
flurry, inside a Wettex shivers in the sink.

Alcohol

A flicker in the rear-view
mirror, maybe of death
I must admit in a flash
looking back I saw
I've lived life as a whore.

Mostly I felt nothing
more than a sly
boredom as life came
tripping from my tongue,
an effulgence

that mostly embarrassed
the men. Often
semi-conscious, tight
with that hard-drinking squint
but ah, they nourished

my skinny soul as I grew
more cynical. The family
man with his boy
in the school play
as some stupid unicorn,

the wife in love
with her cargo, who could
boast of not having
a soul. I was the anti-muse,
the woman

floating there
behind bars, the boy blinking
in cunning innocence.
Syllable by syllable
I wove a picture

just to show what
atrocity could mean – the
fires, the ovens from history
sure, but this one
was for their street.

I mocked with courtesy
and finished up
in churches, reading
poetry, I unremembered dreams.
It ends with a lightening of eyelids.

A future book

Among birds shaped by the stars
I reached through branches,
a levitating feather
difficult to grasp.

The editor pumped for facts,
there's no story here,
just the drifting pinion
and my fingers working

its shaft: I use the lake
as an inkwell, draw
invisible serifs.
Catbirds loop through

the casuarina spray,
I cannot tell you where I am –
somewhere in the bloodstream
is all I can say. My voice

is parched as ink hits the air,
day itself is the only page.
In the lake a bird wades,
its call a swishing of bone.

Side of the creek

Slender gums, flowering spray,
heliotropes at Bobbin Head.
The river calm, smoking.

Each day mangroves die off
a little more, though
their roots shoot upwards

from mud into the sweet air.
A kingfisher lifts up
a cat's eye in its beak,

nearby some fishermen
who do not laugh. At a toll
gate to the national park

a ranger sits in a glass box
drinking his cup of tea;
kingfisher wings sail

through his eyes in an amber
sea of whisky. Out on
the glassy river,

a battered oyster barge
goes purring by. One morning
a mangrove left a drop

of its blood on my
window-pane; the tree ferns
live through bushfires

and massacres, feeding
on time. I caught a tiny egg
as it fell from its branch

and placed it between
my wife's breasts; after a while
a blue chick hatched.

A koel tore the silence apart
with its double wolf-whistle;
the next night, looking

down through monlight
onto the ebb, two huge black
water rats swam off, heading for town.

What I have of faith

If you look out
the window you will see nothing
the willow is flowing nicely

you will be blind
and hear the sound of poetry
read by a woman

who reviews owls, like an owl
split in two by a cat, flying off
in two directions

on this side, a sprig of inkweed
on the other, Tasmanian kelp.
Here language comes out

at night and mixes
with the locals, who knows what
is getting done

aside from talking.
The serious tone is more assuring
well, more than laughter –

for some reason things
change tonight, we hear a muted
thudding, a good night

for the litter of kittens.
Hawks circle the kitchen light,
moths with beaks

come flying out, nothing
surreal. The lawn man walks in
with a glad-bag

dropping feathers; you must
remember to reassemble the goldfinch
before the refreshments.

from

THE LANGUAGE OF OYSTERS
(1997)

Meshing bends in the light

Just under the surface
mullet roll in the current;
their pale bellies catch
the sunken light, the skin
of the river erupts
above purling. The sky
hangs over the boat a wall
of shuddering light
smudging the wings
of a whistling-kite,
mudflats glow
in the developing chemicals,
black crabs hold their
claws up into the light
of the enlarger, yabbies
ping in the drain. A westerly
howls through the
darkroom. The tide
is always working
at the base of the brain.
The turning moon is
up-ended, setting on the silver
gelatin page: a hook
stopped spinning in space.
Owls shuffle their silent wings
and dissolve in the fixer.
Shape words over what you see.
The river flows from your
eyes into the sink, bulrushes
hum with mosquitoes
that speckle the print.
The last riverboat mail-run
scatters letters across
the surface, the ink
runs into the brackish tide.

The language of oysters

Charles Olson sat back in his oyster-shed
working with words – 'mostly in a great
sweat of being, seeking to bind in speed' –

looked at his sheaf of pages, each word
an oyster, culled from the fattening grounds
of talk. They were nurtured from day one,

from the spat-fields to their shucking,
words, oysters plump with life. On Mooney Creek
the men stalk the tides for corruption.

They spend nights in tin shacks
that open at dawn onto our great brown river.
On the right tide they ride out

into the light in their punts, battered slabs
of aluminium with hundred-horse Yamahas on the stern
hammering tightly away, padded by hi-tech –

sucking mud into the cooling systems,
the motors leave a jet of hot piss in their wakes.
These power-heads indicate

the quality of the morning's hum.
The new boys don't wake from dreams
where clinkers crack, where mud sucks them under,

their grandfather's hands fumbling
accurately, loosening the knots. Back
at the bunker the hessian sacks are packed ready

and the shells grow into sliding white foothills.
A freezing mist clenches your fingers,
the brown stream now cold as fire:

plunge in and wash away last night's grog,
in the middle morning, stinging and wanting
the week to fold away until payday.

On the bank, spur-winged plovers stroll in pairs,
their beak-wattle chipped by frost,
each day blinking at the crack of sun.

Stalking for corruption? Signs.
Blue algae drifts through your brother's dream
of Gold Coasts, golf courses. The first settlement.

from

BLACK WATER
Approaching Zukofsky
(1999)

THE STONE CURLEW

The stone curlew

I am writing this inside the head
of a bush stone curlew,
we have been travelling for days

moving over the earth
flying when necessary.
I am not the bird itself, only its passenger

looking through its eyes.
The world rocks slightly as we move
over the stubble grass of the dunes,

at night shooting stars draw lines
across the velvet dark
as I hang in a sling of light

between the bird's nocturnal eyes.
The heavens make sense, seeing this way
makes me want to believe

words have meanings,
that Australia is no longer a wound
in the side of the earth.

I think of the white settlers
who compared the curlew's song
to the cries of women being strangled,

and remember the poets who wrote
anthropomorphically as I sing softly
from the jelly of the stone curlew's brain.

The pheasant-tailed jacana

The canoe wings its way up stream,
a school of garfish scatter
around lily-pads, streaking

silver pencils, scribbling nonsense;
their gut-sacks translucent,
alive with insect larvae, calligraphic ink.

Green and difficult, wet
feathers trailing, the jacana draws
lines of cobweb through sunlight

picking off spinning dragonflies;
air bubbles up from the mouth
of a lungfish under its surface stepping feet.

Maybe the image of the jacana
comes to the insane remembering Jesus.
Up here in the jungle

we see flowers glowing,
smelling as sweet in the fist of a stumped
drunk, grumbling back

at his own face reflected
in a flowing sheet of creek.
Leaping back into the picture, stepping out

with its flag-tail held high
for no reason but instinct pinging from its eyes
drawing in shapes we cannot know.

The great knot

Alterant birds, alterant words
and Bunting's descant on a madrigal,
Zukofsky's 'descrying black-hellebore

white white double flowered
marsh-mallow mallow-rose
snowstorm sea-hollyhock'

and you're dancing with words in particular.
This bird's a traveller, summers
in north-eastern Siberia,

winters in southern China
and has vagrants that fly to Australia.
Zukofsky's flowers are words in bloom

strung out along the song lines,
the great knot as tricky as whisky
running along whisky-coloured shores

where clear water laps granite
and salt water foams on the sandstone.
Its shadow shoots over lagoons

rancid with verbiage in disintegration
as it tries to describe the sink ponds of paper mills,
factories discharging, alterant poems.

Arctic jaeger

This bird comes between the light
and your reading, hang-glides
in the corner of your eye, a pirate

with a feather in its cap – a sly con
riding the breath of your best line;
flying straight out of Olson's delirium tremens

hangs around with dead things
under its wing; heavier than a night heron
like a loose-winged falcon:

take its shape to mean blood sport
on our terms. Lines drawn from the breath,
one flash of meaning following

another, a bad draft tangled in its claw
a quote from Cohen's *The Future*
in its bill – this bird cuts out descriptions

its flight over bleak oceans
tells no story, its white plumage a flying page
written in a language not endangered.

The whimbrel

All beak, jabbing sand to pierce
the sand-coloured shell of a ghost crab:
poets who love this creature
know it as a bird made of words
that will disappear if spoken.
It runs the beach at Skippy Rock, Augusta,
where it pecks for arthropods,
yet when it visits England it eats berries.
It comes in pairs or in thousands,
its call a series of bubbling trills
that rise and fall with the tide, it holds a sickle
bill above the rushes and sings
until something happens.
A poet of sand, it draws calligraphic marks
along the shores of great ponds in Manchuria
that ornithologists claim to understand.
I watched one tumble from the sky
one afternoon landing in a mangrove tree,
it sat there through the rise of an orange moon.
L=A=N=G=U=A=G=E poets
are doomed should they decipher
the song of the sandy whimbrel.

The southern skua

The skua flew into our heads in 1968 –
a new kind of poetry, a scavenging predator
frequently attacking humans,
flying through the streets of seaside towns,
foraging with seagulls. This bird
has few predators. One was found
in Tasmania, its beak embedded in the skull
of a spotted quoll, dragged
into a clearing by devils. They form clubs
and proclaim their territory
by various displays and loud aggressive calls;
they are agile metaphysicians,
sweeping along lines of projective verse,
echoing each other's songs.
Although the skua breeds on Black Mountain
it is migratory and dispersive, its call
a series of low quacks and thin whinnying squeals.
They are omnivorous and critical creatures;
animal liberationists never mention
the habits of skua. If you read skua poetry, beware:
one could fly out from the page
and change the expression on your face.

TROPIC BIRD

When the light slants against the tide

We arrive by boat, rowing ourselves home.
The tide pulls conversation from our mouths,
the backyard is full of wind blowing
through the lonely heads of our family.

Sometimes my sister swings out from the tree
and talks to the crows tearing at fish heads,
she draws black feathers in the sand pit
using the dark mud from the riverside.

Oh this life will soon pass,
says our mother on her way to Church,
and then where will you be, you two with your birds?
The turkey blowing bubbles in its drink trough.

I stare at the bottom of our rowboat
for hours, until gashes and holes appear in the clinkers;
I row out into the flowing tide
and yet the boat stays at my mother's feet.

We row together, my sister works an oar
I try to balance mine with her stroking;
nothing seems to satisfy our desire for flight,
every attempt we make to swing out into the light fails.

Drum of fire

Out the back my father's burning off –
drums of scrap, the lead casing
dripping from the copper wire,
toxic black smoke billowing into the air
each weekend, the lead trickling
down, molten rivulets spitting fire,
becoming deformed ingots. His
fuming shadow looming over
neat rows of vegetables.
Weekdays I went back to school at night,
cutting through the alphabet,
torching examination papers, drunk
on fumes of kerosene, my fingers
marking strokes. At morning
assembly we sang the national anthem flat
with deadpan faces – I blew
into a flute for a whole term but wept
each night over my arithmetic
homework – then down to the Police Boys
boxing with the bigger kids until my
eyebrow bled too much. In the park
I flew with rainbow lorikeets
and hung upside down in the branches
of flowering coral trees. I sucked
nectar with them and stole their feathers;
prowled back lanes with a pair
of parrot's claws dried into spiky stars
in my pockets. Back home I'd stare
into my father's drum of flames –
conjuring images of the new Ford Thunderbirds
that came purring through our suburb,
and found no meaning in my father's fire
as he stashed another ton of scrap copper wire.

In the open air

The beach is high with the smell of kelp –
kids play with it, hanging loose
garlands through their hair,
skin seems to smoke, sunburn lotion
runs and streaks down their limbs.

A young man flicks his towel like a whip,
the family dog salivates
as ice cream melts and dribbles
over the feet of his bright yellow friend.
On the edge of the blue world a ship

moves slowly out to sea.
A mother drags a little girl to the slow surf,
she digs in, screams in tantrum.
These people with multicoloured picnics
move across the sand in a kind of journey –

maybe a pilgrimage, who knows what
they're doing, what it's for. These days I write
about it, retracing a childhood, sorting out
this hell from that. A cuttlefish bone
eaten away from within, a cracked sea slug cone.

At Berry's Bay

A boy crawls through dawn's beams
of light illuminating the black
stumps of an old coal-wharf, the air's full
of oil and tar fumes. As he climbs
he thinks of the chain of milky puddles
along the shore, each one marbled
with chemical rainbows – on a slack
tide they look inviting –

yet how that trapped water stung
and inflamed the fine cuts made by pulling
black mussels from the pylons
with his hands. He looks
out from a dark corner in the hub
of the great wharf; out there across
the harbour, the Wedding Cakes, flashing
their red and green navigation code

are still visible as a morning breeze bends
the fading reflections across the wake
from a bullnosed tug. His pocket
holds a fishing line, twenty yards
of Japanese catgut wound around a cork
with six tiny long-shanked hooks
embedded in one end; he spreads out his bait
on a plank: flesh from the black mussels,

four green prawns in neat segments.
Underneath the surface
of the smooth oiled-over tide, his dream fish
hover, fantail leatherjackets, their
dorsal spikes upright, nail-clipper teeth
pruning filaments of the pylon's weed;
the turquoise and orange on their tails, florets
of tissue, pulsing chevrons.

Swimming out with Emmylou Harris

A long curved horizon, the hazel-
coloured tide and Lion Island
going by. A CD player skips
on the line *A quarter moon*

in a ten cent town, on the swell
our wake shatters the reflection
of the real moon. We cut
through the sound of swimming,

the meaningless joy of living,
the random punishment of birth.
The song says, we all live up to what
we get – out here you believe

whoever writes the script.
Yesterday is reflected back by the moon;
mothers wash the sickly
smell from a dozen ruined shirts

every Saturday afternoon. Wives
turn their heads. There's an old grey
stingray spread-eagled across
the front of the chicken run,

three crows hop around it, the breeze
ruffling their satin collars.
They plunge their black beaks
into the lukewarm flesh. Emmylou,

your sweet holy music drifts
through the new curtains,
your song folds itself around the shack
filling the backyard, flowing through

our days, out on the back veranda
where Old Dutch sits slumped two days
into his latest coma. Sweet Lord,
sweet poison, sweet, sweet music.

Tropic bird

(Lord Howe Island 1996)

Wakes from nimbus cut to streaks
by the clipped volcanic peaks
mingle with an orange sky, the colour
of parrot-fish gut. Monsoon

time, nothing's quite right,
people drink or sleep or drift about.
On my deck chair's arm a tumbler
of gin has sucked in a dragonfly.

I drink myself sober as they say.
All that happens is my past
oozes through its pack of black jokes
and disasters. During *Under the Volcano*

I sucked bourbon through a straw
from a milkshake carton, at 4am
eating handfuls of icecream
I tried to soothe a hangover that went on

for a decade. I watched three
Siamese cats and as many marriages
sink with the fish. Always fish.
Tight water in black pools, moonlight

etching outlines of game-fishing boats
onto my brain. Moored in slots,
fat with money yet taut, their
trimmings set to kill. I worked them,

sharpened hooks for high-rollers,
sewing my special rigs.
Bridles for bonito, live bait that
trailed the barbed viridian in our wake.

On the arm of my bamboo chair the glass
of gin is blossoming. The sky opens
and in sails, on black-edged wings,
a white, gracefully inhuman, tropic bird.

Kingfishers appearing

A circle of blue falls over
a kingfisher, an exercise in ink control.
Its flight out of mist
plunges me into the day.
I pull the tide in empty, feel again
the hollow pit in my chest, craving
the uncertainty of fog.

Waking beside you, always
dropped from nowhere into this bed
how does it happen? The sheets
full of light, my head riddled with dark.
Grace is a blazing radiance
as I reach over, my arms full
of branches, where the kingfisher

does not alight, where the mist
doesn't hang. In a climate of silence
a space, a pit of indigo
filled by the flight of the bird,
my life these fluttering pages falling
through the kingfisher's blue life, turning
white with their prey.

Crows in afternoon sunlight

How close can a human get to a crow,
how much do we know about them?
It's good to know we'll never read their brains,
never know what it means to be a crow.

All those crow poems are about poets –
none of them get inside the crow's head,
preen or rustle, let alone fly on crow wings.

No one knows what it is to sing crow song.

Five crows hop and stand around
the fish I have left for them on the wharf.
If I move their eyes follow me. I stand still
and they pick up a fish, test its weight,

then ruffle their feathery manes and shine.

These black bird shapes outlined by the light,
behind them the river flowing out, the light
changing – soon it will be night

and they will be gone. Before that
I praise crows.

The gathering light

Morning shines on the cowling of the Yamaha
locked onto the stern of the boat
spears of light shoot away
from the gun-metal grey enamel.
Now I wait for God to show
instead of calling him a liar.

I've just killed a mulloway –
it's eighty-five pounds, fifty years old –
the huge mauve-silver body trembles in the hull.

Time whistles round us, an invisible
flood tide that I let go
while I take in what I have done.
It wasn't a fight, I was drawn to this moment.
The physical world drains away
into a golden calm.

The sun is a hole in the sky, a porthole –
you can see turbulence out there,
the old wheeling colours and their dark forces –
but here on the surface of the river
where I cradle the great fish in my arms
and smell its pungent death, a peace
I have never known before –
a luminous absence of time, pain,
sex, thought – of everything but light.

APPROACHING ZUKOFSKY

Meaning

A black summer night, no moon, the thick air
drenched with honeysuckle and swamp gum.

     In a pool of yellow torchlight
on a knife-blade, the brand name
                     Hickey Miffle –
I give in to meaninglessness, look up
try to read smudges of ink
                a live squid squirts
across the seats – now the smell of the river hones
an edge inside my brain,
     the night sky, Mallarmé's first drafts.

Who can I talk to now that you have left
the land of the living? The sound of more words.

The moon rolls out from the side of a mountain,
and I decide to earn the rent;

     the net pours into a thick chop,
a line of green fire running before the moon's light –

Does four-inch mesh have anything to say tonight?

The mulloway might think so if they could –
Ah, Wordsworth, why were you so human?

     On Friday nights I fork out comfort,
but tonight I work with holes, with absence.

I feed out a half-mile of mesh pulling the oars;
this comes once a life, a song without words
     a human spider spinning a death web

across the bay. Alcohol, my friend my dark perversion,
here's to your damage:
     who do you think you are?

My mother the belly dancer, my father Silence,
     my house that repeats itself wherever I go.

The night heron

Midnight, my mind's full of ink tonight,
I'm drawing up some endings to make
a few last marks. Life's complete.
You're just part of the mix,
a pain cocktail, a dash of white spirit,
some pulvules of dextropropoxyphene
swallowed with black label
apple juice, as I cut and paste my past.

Life is sweet. Out there the night,
the stars in technicolor, a half-moon –
two half-moons, the black branches
of a mangrove tree. Jasmine's
heavy in the hot air, I feel all right
even here suspended in a humid room
with another summer to get through.
I write down words, they all seem fake,

so I crack them open. A night
writing letters to the future and the past –
if you could look into the present
you might see this pudgy figure at the desk
throwing back double shots of gin,
fumbling for cigarettes and a light
writing the word 'political' in a black
thin calligraphy. Wearing a pair of digital

blinkers set on zero. Outside the night
heron swings in from the heavens
and cuts through the aluminium light –
see its cream underwings, the grey breast,
the grey overcoat, watch it hit the pocket
of hot air, listen as it wheels on silence,
glides into the black calm above the swamp
and lands collecting in the creek.

The bunker

(for Joseph Guglielmi)

My walls are made of fish scales, we slip
through words, fissures, cracks
in the radiance. Outside the slot of air

that is our window, phrases
from French and English fleck the night
with whatever we are.

We expect poems to catch
what words can't; talk of life breaks in,
filleting the code, a syllable's blade,

a fish, a cold hand – so we create
sonnets of skin, little bunkers for emergencies,
spikes of meaning inside them

parting the river of words.
In times of peace we drift down rivers
through countries and into oceans.

We fish for sirens, then discuss fishing
with them – it's a fine thing to do
in the real sea with living fish to kill and eat,

our words lures spinning
in their heads. Though once you start
thinking about it you're sunk,

there's no simulacrum, you can't construct
meanings for fishing – you can
fashion a fish trap though,

weld wire into a cage or hoop – but there's no
welding the wires in your head.
Take some flesh and thread it onto

a chemically sharpened hook, the offshore
Gamakatsu – is there any vernacular
clarity in that? At night under the stars

we just do it, poems flow –
next morning the talk seems stupid
as you stand, water dribbling through the holes

in your big dipper, about to be
rust – more scales forming –
in the gammer of sun.

The white abyss

After a life, the next decade
is a concept I must comprehend –
Time, wrote Augustine, is some kind of trick.

He asked his God to forgive him
for thinking along those lines,
it had to be done,

What happens next? Outside
Hell smoulders as usual
inside, electricity and words.

Everything exists to end in the book.

I live in Mallarmé's head for days
nothing happens and this
is paradise, thoughts
unfold instead of flowers, abstract and warm.

I have not experienced a grief
as devastating as the black abyss
the death of Anatole left –
this is a corner of the head I prefer
not to revisit

when I go back the intensity
of the experience of loss leaves me empty.

This is a death then, a blank
where no thought flowers, a pit of black
tideless water, where no fish kill.
Here you realise you can live through anything,
stripped, without a head, your soul
shown up for the dark joke souls are.

Then you begin to understand Augustine.

Approaching Zukofsky

(for John Kinsella)

We read wings of the blue bonnets
and mixed parrot with talk, their colours
ink for a new language. Our heads
tilted into the dusk as we listened

to their beaks, living jigsaws
in the vibrating atmosphere.
Pine cones tumbled in a code pulled
through the accounting surf.

There was a forest of spotted gums
fringed with a scrub of woolly butts.
In this text we deciphered the brilliant red
on the chest of the king parrot

as an emblem or version of paradise.
Were we thrown by the taste
of inferno stuck in our craw? The thick air
supported moths and their

powdery calligraphy, and off on
the outskirts of hearing, their croaking.
We scratched lyrics in parrot
and danced the stump-hop.

Our translations were the husks
the birds tossed from the oily rape-seed.
We itched with what flits through
the parrot's brain as we entered

that counterfeit hell. Each level offered
some form of music, in the midst
of an interminable fugue we found
ourselves speaking in the endless now –

in a lust for attention we figured
every word in that blown puzzle of air:
what could we do but listen and plan?
When the way turns up, we will wade through

lagoons of music, words sticking
our dreams feathery; each
discovery a permission. New beaks
will open cages in landscapes frosted by white

polyurethane. Aleatorical bulrushes
will part, vertical winds rise and float us
across. On the other side we will drop
our wrecked lyrics onto tender grasses.

As we stumble onto the word meat
it will shake off the dew from its wings
then wobble into a description of cannibalism.
Afterwards we will listen

as it ravages itself calling for more
with the last bit of its tongue. All this in
an art book. We are stuck in this painting,
necks of oil holding up our heads

so that we can see back to the time
our world was a blank. My finger is pecking
out a final draft of this life. Outside
the frame, the trees are loaded

with a great flock of night parrots, they eat
black moths in duplicate. We sang
parrot with them but how were we to know
our mythic birds were carnivores,

their blue bonnets, stained with ink, fading
in the heat? We flash our heads, our fingers
feather the keyboard, we hear their triangular
tongues thick with music of alarm.

Black water

I took Robert Duncan in my grandfather's skiff
rowing across Mooney Creek
words hummed around our heads

The trees are speaking on the far shore
we'll never get there in time
the pages of books swim upstream

we study words growing on them
The time will come and you will turn
the present a breeze that passes

sweeps up carrying the odor
The Mower is creating as he moves through
the rushes looking for glowworms

Words little warm animals of air
words growing and teaming over the mudflats
This river has no bends

this river is not an actual river yet
this water has burnt its right of way into sandstone
Great sheets of it slide by on either side

parting and taking the flotsam
The Mower creates 'for she my mind hath so displaced
that I shall never find my home'

Marvell was calling from the mangroves
our souls crows gliding down to eat the words
time created endless bends

the river was never the same
that night Duncan gathered the southern stars
into his being the black water plopping with fat mullet

DAYBOOK FOR EURYDICE

Daybook for Eurydice

written to illustrate Gria Shead's 'Just Another Day in Paradise'

A sprig of delphinium (2 pm)

She saw hoops in his eyes, behind the brown
cordage of opaque veins, wheels of light.
I believed him. In this fashionable precinct
there is a café where the pagans hang out –

the perpendicular city shoots up and the sky
is smudged across the window, a bevy of road-peckers
rule the roost but don't worry, if anyone
walks in on us maybe they'll skid into

an imbroglio and have some gratuitous fun.
If gender is a foreign language, let's drop
expectations, sleight of word and be impetuous.

Take this sprig of delphinium, my chatterbox,
our lives will change.

Raining italics (4 pm)

He travels heavy, lopsided, slanting home,
leaving behind the scene in the café.
What's pertinent now? What type of flower
will shoot from his eye when he endeavours

to create his paradise? He walks the streets
of the inner city enduring his limbo, calm as a sentence
not including weather. When he trundles
through the gates he knows there will

be phosphor-headed floozies and acceptance.
He remembers his mother pruning geraniums;
he played in her garden with his hoop

and watched the rainbow. Time is fascinating
yet vile. The rain creates acrid fumes.

The transcribed hoop (6 pm)

We are lines in a hand-coloured lithograph.
We watch a hoop trying to bowdlerise itself.
Strange markings. These lines have been
forced onto the paper, you can read the result

of the printer's pathetic yodelling – in the small hours
he practised his calligraphy, his imagination's
gyrating tonnage. His scribbling was a fine
exercise until he decided to transcribe it.

What his ebullient inspiration amounted to was
simply heavy doodling. Every day he said: tomorrow.
He'd frame it up and make a presentation –

a Valentine, he'd tear his chest apart. Self-critical to a t,
he rolled it up, posting off a tube.

The visible, the untrue (1 pm)

This room has existed for all these years in
Edmund Spenser's head, a gnome works
there on an etching of a hummock. His
first sketch was drawn from life one day

as he lay out by the juniper attending to those
details that nature did omit, breaking bread mixed in
with Edmund's 'substance base.' True Jonathan
does some kind of a dance and raves.

The Faerie Queen is a drag show bedecked and scored
with synthetic cloth and acrylic glitter, they eat
the drumsticks of the bird of paradise:

their great ideals have been mollified by grim lust,
their geodesic discotheque is held together by art alone.

The bower of bliss (1 am)

Birds, voices, instruments, winds, waters
all agree: the windpipe created a melodious tone
as the blade sunk home. Although sorcery
is not in fashion it worked. The mask of Cupid fell,

revealing a man without a hat, a murderous
swine cold as a jobfish. If we translate the circuitous
murmuring of hoops bowled along, if we
squint, a picture will form from the sounding:

it will turn out to be the blond woman
from *Blonde On Blonde,* the sad-eyed lady herself –
she has a rendezvous tomorrow, under a juniper tree

with a landscape painter. They'll exchange sketches.
Outside on the street drunks are shadow-boxing neon.

Nothing on the mind (3 am)

The gnome's Akubra is part of his head.
He drinks Jack & Coke – at last they've come up
with an alcoholic robot. Let me tell you
ambition leads to imitation oak.

The weight of eyes rides on my cheeks,
until blotchy flowers become thoughts
feeding by brain; venomous butterflies flit
through my eardrums. When the limits fall away,

brightness flares about, there is no shade
nothing but illumination on a sea of drink.
Philosophers I swallowed undigested swim in circles,

bronze-whalers of the intellect, you can't dream
in this slipstream of blood. Your punishment is to think.

Our different versions (4 am)

Everybody thinks they've been in hell too long,
it's the quality of the shades you meet.
I'm fond of the ones who say we're underground,
maybe it's the language of the inferno

that keeps it bearable. Or the letters home.
Then his voice over-riding the morning:
I'll give you one last song that will explain everything.
Some girl's been walking naked in the bedroom,

softly howling for an hour. She's not out of it,
just a bit tight, who wants to spoil the night?
Hell has no location. There's a swirl of information

and we notice the details on the edges. Stay hear me sing.
An old song is scratching the tissue of the drum.

The sepia hummock (10.30 am)

She threw open the window and light dappled
the furniture, it made the artifact
leachy and banal. It came in a tube.
The fellow from Edmund Spenser's head

had sent her his etching of a hummock, it wasn't
pushing the envelope of landscape, it was
simply a weird twist in the narrative. Can you
stalk yourself? Her morning fell apart,

she forgot to feed the baby barramundi in
their tank for the restaurant, the dish-washer
imploded. Simple tasks became operatic. A man

on a talkback radio show was grunting. She turned
the volume up. The amplifier blew a tweeter.

She speaks, language falls apart

I cannot remain silent and outside time
any longer, this city just repeats itself
wars and people come and go. Pigeons and rats
stay the same, the blue-bar fans his tail

and does his two-step with sound effects,
in the rain his breast throws out its rainbow, he bobs
and runs and gets reassuring rejections. I want
to focus on some particular time and place,

drink Split Rock mineral water and talk.
Wasted, wasted on time, wasted eloquence,
rhetoric can get you out of hell, barbaric song

can brace your soul, can be equivocal as pigeon talk.
All I am is words, human song, a noise that edges in.

At the ferry, the tide

Who is Eurydice under the stars? One night I stood
naked on a pylon of the wharf – as the ferries
came close, we'd dive just in front of them,
and as we swam, the water flowed through us.

Particles, we streamed through the
symbiotic tide – our cells, phosphorescent,
came up churned and laughing from that
dangerous wake. No Eurydice but playing out

the myth: there's a boatman waiting where
the memory fades. Our lovers, drunk, sang for tourists,
fluking coins with the drugs and wine.

It was bracing to live in that paradise
as lucidity cut through the wax.

Song

We all know the past can't interleave
with now, I fly into this. Now outside
the harbour flows into morning –
walking on sand, swimming in air,

the texture of flowers exploding with satin
bowerbirds, rainbow lorikeets and the
seduction of perfumes, the tides
full of mullet bouncing from glassy

water, leatherjackets sucking at pylons,
butterflies in the magnolias, kids flying a kite
and that airliner shimmering against the red sky.

My love, today I'll catch you a silver dory
and tonight, grill it with lemon and a pinch of salt.

Coda: the Nightjar

Seems weird a bird Aristotle talked about
lives here, the nightjar
Aegotheles cristatus, crested goatsucker,

under the city in a deserted railway station,
a great white cave. The electricity
has been cut and it is completely dark.

She flies out along the air ducts
up into the city's towers,
eating moths along the way.

The nightjar, according to Aristotle,
would fly out over the country
and find goats to drink from their teats.

Eurydice flies up from under the ground
and moves through the penthouses,
her white wings stroking polished atmosphere

going from bed to bed, changing form,
listening for her lover's song.

CREON'S DREAM

After Brett Whiteley

We're on this looping road, it's narrow
and the car's fast and expensive,
too fast considering we've downed a few.
There's a woman singing Bob Dylan well,

too well as the line about what you want
cuts through the climate control
mixing the smell of jonquils with hot
bodies. Things are looking dangerous.

Then suddenly the waters are before us,
the surface a black raw silk all ironed out
and drifting through a fishy light.
We are still in the car and quibbling

as a wild duck makes an evanescent wake
across the phosphorous tide. The woman turns
to Brett and says: is this decadence? No man,
he mutters, just reflected glory up shit creek.

The art critic

Out here on the windy stream the lecturer
weathers his dream, his little boat
moored by a loquat tree shuffling its yellow
fruit. For months the papers have

hovered over his bed. Tonight he marks
them, on Fridays he writes his piece on art.
His boat is a mild addiction, a darker
side where he seeks atonement

for a fissure he hides. The shape
of a black mussel picked from a pylon:
he throws it into a pot then eats the flesh
of his small sin. If art can serve

a theory it will sing. When night comes,
the gorge out there will brim with mist.
He will cough wisps of it at dawn.
As he tries to gargle the song of a bullfinch

feathers will float out from the bristles
on his chin. In his head there's a mallet
he lets thud through his dreams, but after
the marking he will flower, and the students

won't even know. A newspaper hits a mat
on his verandah prickled with frost.
His piece is published. The sun will strike,
and the bullfinch sing through his fountain pen.

Creon's dream

The old hull's spine shoots out of the mud-flat,
a black crooked finger pointing back to the house.
On the dead low the smell of the mangroves.

The river seeps through the window, the books
are opened out on the desk. When the first breeze
hits the curtain the cats scatter.

It could be dawn for all I know, concentration
wanders through Creon's words to Antigone
Go to the dead and love them – okay so they live as

long as I do – what else can I make of it?
The bright feathers from a crimson rosella lie
in clumps on the floor with a pair of broken wings.

In the dark I try to write and remember the zoo
I played in as a child. There was a balding sedated lion
and a wedge-tailed eagle hunched on a dead

tree in a cage; they threw it dead rabbits
in 1953. The whooping cranes side-
stepped the concrete ponds and whooped all night.

The blue heron flaps across the river in my head,
poddy mullet hanging from its tight beak.
Ah, dead fish, the old black crow, the sick pelican.

I pad the room, out there mangroves are pumping up
the putrid air, life goes on. At the zoo they
still throw the animals dead meat, the big cats

are bred in labs where they lock the albino
freaks away. I pace the kitchen: where are the books,
who reads the poems? I take a drink, ribbonfish

swim across my pages, I shake my head but they swim on –
in low flocks, chromium ribbons, they fly under
the river herding up the poddy mullet,

rippling the surface, as the tawny frogmouth knows.
The books have gone, the spoonbills wade in
with whitebait skipping ahead of them,

channel-billed cuckoo come swooping after the crows,
flying low over the water, calling their mates,
dipping their hooked beaks into the moving chrome.

I sleep in broken snatches and dream nothing.
Mosquitoes suck at my cheeks and empty bottles
clutter the verandah, the books are in darkness

but the sandy whimbrels finger the pages, words
dissolve, waves of the dead arrive in dreams.
Out there the black finger points to the mouth

of the river, where the dead are heading, they
move over the window glass. The extinct fins move
the fingers of my grandfather, mending nets,

the dead friends sing from invisible books. The heron
pick the blood-shot eyes from my father's terrible
work in the kilns and the darkness is complete.

from

MULBERRY LEAVES

(2001)

Éventail: for Mery in Paris

Writing this in sepia ink on a Japanese fan,
pain slants my calligraphy
this way, sex just under the cap of my skull.

Dreams taunt your existence
as you swish by in raw silk
until the words I use lose meaning

and my best lines twang like limp
old lace. This metaphor thick with blood
trembles as my mind approaches the blank

folds in the rice paper, writing
on your arms, this scrawl scrolling
through you, each letter a link in the chain

between my head and the bed, a text
of splintering syllables in which
time comes apart, pricking your skin –

the joke's our meaning, gnarled
with the word-knots coming undone
where your breast shines with the sepia

ink and the sheets blot out thinking.
Smudged with love, your bum's a haze
of lavender oil as I rub this in.

On not seeing Paul Cézanne

(Sydney 1999)

I think of the waste, the long
years of not believing the
tongue pretending

in the midst of words
to speak, to keep walking
that bend in the road

I cursed myself for not having spoken

The blank sheets of air could have added

Words smudged out and revised with a colour

stroked instead of butting
coming to the shape by layers, stumbling
in from the corners and rubbing out the hard light

The countless fish flapping on boards
Have they just disappeared?
there's no way

back to the water to catch
again that possible
colour

Outside the window in the black night
mosquitoes gather under floodlights on the pontoon
until the empty westerly blows

Everything that matters comes together
slowly, the hard way, with the immense and tiny details,
all the infinite touches, put down onto nothing –

each time we touch
it begins again, love quick brush strokes
building up the undergrowth from the air into what holds

Symbolism

At Uladulla
a bittern puffs out its neck feathers,
head between wings –

slits of its eyes tight in the wind
flinging sand, hammering grains of stone
against it.

Our bird of words falls apart –
its wings without vowels,
its head empty of tough money.

O bittern, come off it, talk to us
about when we were young: that first
kiss hissing as she bit my tongue.

Elizabeth Bishop in Tasmania

The hopscotch map on the pavement
puzzled her at first, a boy mucking
around with a hoop caught her eye
and she put them together

as a sharp new drink. A wizard with flowers
no good with bereavement, she
continuously topped up her bright stanzas
and tucked her emotions away

in print. The critics write about her
scrupulous control, her management
of traditional forms alongside her *vers libre* –
hardly her style in life itself,

where she found oblivion in tides
of drink. She said she wanted
'closets, closets and more closets!' She set
sail for Tasmania once a year, when the moon

was full. Nobody knew where she ended
up, her subterfuge being her poetry, which gave
only invisible clues. She was a true
Tasmanian. Bring me

flying fish on a crinkled ocean, seahorse
and Patagonian toothfish: the icy crags
turn pink tonight – there's a kissing of flesh
on flesh as the eyes dim and the blackbirds sing.

The upland sandpiper

*The Upland Sandpiper scrapes into the list of Australian birds on
the strength of but one record. The bird, 'Shot by an old sportsman,
during the snipe seasons of 1848, near the water reservoir in the vicinity
of Sydney', was sent to John Gould in London by the Committee
of Superintendence of the Australian Museum in Sydney.*

JOHN DOUGLAS PRINGLE

When it comes to earth it lands on airfields.
Maybe it remembers its original haunts,
the American prairies – the bird
books say it is 'gregarious at all seasons,
though often encountered alone'.
The upland sandpiper breeds in Alaska
and winters in South America; this bird
is the totem animal of the Australian poet
Anthony Lawrence. It makes only long-distance
calls to James Dickey, knowing it would
be shot by him on sight. Although
this bird is a distant relative of the
stone curlew it does not have a square head
and its eyes are the colour of live bait;
it shoots out of existence if forced onto
paper; some say it can read the handwriting
of the reeds in a pond in Clarksburg, Ontario.
Another theory is that John Gould
invented it – so that this bird exists *only*
on paper. Recently I heard a lyrebird
mimicking its call, a series of mellow
whistling trills, echoing over the incoming
tide on the Hawkesbury River.

The Hudsonian godwit

Although it breeds in Hudson Bay,
it winters in South America.
However, a lone vagrant godwit
was found at Kooragang Island
in New South Wales before
the Christmas of 1982 – word
spread quickly and many observers
travelled to Newcastle to see it.
They are still searching. This
Australian godwit's call – *toy, toy, toy* –
was recorded and this recording
has been compared to the work
of Phil Spector. Its markings are
complex and beautiful, with
prominent white supercilium,
dorsum deep grey with each feather
fringed white, its underparts mainly
soot-grey. It is a bird for objectivists.
It wades through the shallows,
its bill making rapid stitching motions
as it sews together its own wake.
The godwit's cryptic markings
make it a perfect object for the similes
of Australia's 'greatest imagist' – but
don't look, you won't find it.

The cow bird

This is not poetry. Its turkey-head
has a craw that produces crap – its
chicks get covered in a stench
you could compare to the breath
of an alcoholic cane toad that's feasted
on a bucket of rancid pork. The
descriptive drift throws up this
internationalist, the hoatin
(pronounced *what-seen*), lives
on the banks of the Orinoco River,
flowing through the central plains
of Venezuela. Its young dive-bomb
into the stream from their nests
overhead, swim underwater
and then pull themselves back into
the trees with clawed wing-tips.
The idea of these creatures has been
known to drive scientific investigators
crazy: infesting the imaginations
of phytochemists from within,
creating themselves on the dark
whims of their hosts, parachuting in
through the eyes. Good students
have fried their brains contemplating
the mating habits of the cow bird –
they are, however, pure joy to
confessional poets, who weave them
in as tropes as they write poems
concerning their wedding night,
when they consummated their bliss
oozing the milk of *What-Seens*.

Memory walks

Ideas of memory walks
replace our need for narrative
Our heads flicker projecting their stories

There's a boat at the end of each tale
and the weary can just paddle out
onto the stream

water sparkling with minerals good enough to drink
Each stroke of the oar stains it
with the inky clouds of thinking

Here we come across the node
of the fractured sentence that indicates
an overload so we dump our ballast of loves

There's a couple of lives
and the brave among us can choose both
The consequences are there each morning

flaring away in the bathroom mirror
staring over the coffee and toast
the space where lovers come clean

about their strolls
and what they scratched on public walls
the night before

Reaching light

Where was it we left from?
We say the journey's up, but maybe

memory sinks deeper.
Our journey so far

has been quiet, the only
incident being that rock dislodged

as he spun around on his heel.
What was that stuff – brimstone?

The first slice of sunlight glanced off
a slab of dark marble that turned to glow.

His back moved ahead of me –
his curls, shoulders,

that neck. What new bone was he inventing
in his shuffling head, what chance

that a doorway would appear and then a house?
The dark supported me, comfortably

behind me, a cradle woven from
demon hair. As I rose

and climbed toward day, his turning head,
those eyes – strips of memory,

silver tides, moons rising over the
rim of the world –

brought back the day we were married,
standing in fine rain, then escaping from family,

sex by a rolling surf in a high wind, velvet
heavens and the stars omens:

calendars, clocks, zodiacs –
straight, bent signs.

Coal & Candle Creek

(for Peter Minter)

Our boat *Swamp Harrier* floating into the light
thrown by council generators

earth-movers lumbering at No Parking signs

free to drift about at 2am
through closed waters, fishing

for creatures swimming upright in deep water –

do we exist? The men on shore

throwing little balls of light at us are cursing,
the green fire of chemical lures

the light-eating hairtails with their bent teeth
prawn heads crawling into the battery-case

a line of trevally piss

maybe we exist as post-christians
searching the night for light eating fish to catch

or send back to their salty abyss

maybe Saint Augustine still loved his wife
who was sent away for being no good

for his holy career

Spring night

(for Kevin Hart)

In the darkness beyond the swimming pool,
flying foxes beat through the air, the cat crouches
in the double shadow of the palm tree.
An amateur fisherman flicks a lure

at the racks of oysters near the shore,
then gives up and swigs a bottle of whisky.
Ah, the way that first drink braces.
A motorboat roars by – no lights –

the black river swallows it, leaving behind
a swirl of fumes. The surface
reflects the glow from our house, as we listen
to the long hooting call of a nightjar.

Stars fracture the sky with light.
The cat keeps playing with these weird
marsupials, the hook wound on my finger
stings like hell – Jesus

didn't walk the water in this river valley.

Domestic shuffle

A bike with one wheel buckled, the other
slowly turning in the wind, feathers
scattered around its circumference, caged
finches squeaking near the sandpit where the

children play. When a woman in the laundry
doorway starts flapping her wings, the little
girl chases the cat, the boy starts yelling –
it's morning, it's still in the morning.

Button your lips and swallow, keep
those words from rumbling out. They're from the
Bible: turn the page in your head
and say to yourself *forgive*, for God's sake

forgive and forget, there's nothing to be said.
A hand lashes out, words making a noise,
and suddenly your mother's hand's slapping your face
hard. You can't remember the actual sting, the shock

and pain the hand inflicted. Now forgive
its meaning: put your hand into water as hot
as you can bear it – the throbbing will fade as the water
cools, like poison from a red rock cod.

Nothing repeats itself, not even heat. Time
is not time, music not music, even Wagner's
Tristan und Isolde playing from the quarterdeck,
even this domestic shuffle that continues as we speak.

Father's Day

I cart home sugarbags of coke from the gasworks.
My hands smudge the cream-painted icebox.
My father throws spuds on the fire,
sending sparks up the flue.

On the hill outside, trucks growl and strip their gears.
I imagine the peach-faced finches of Madagascar.
After tea, Dad slumps in his chair, tall brown
bottles standing empty on the table.

At school each day I fail my tests.
My mother's face hardens when I try to speak.
She irons starch into my sister, from her
straight black hair to her box-pleats.

Outside, cuckoo chicks squawk from a magpie's nest.
The hedge man's finished clipping the hedges along our street.
My brothers bob down to do their homework, into the
learning stream, heading for their lives, biting the heads off words.

Letter to James McAuley

Looking at the full tide slide
out tonight by the bridge lights,
I think of your lyrics – black,
cool and cynical – lines that
come into my mind automatically

staining the edges of memories
already darkened by things I've done.
A smattering of tailor chop at whitebait
as the tide runs out, a fishhawk glides
through the last of the daylight

above the glowing bridge.
Everything is hungry – animals
eat each other, humans feed on darkness
and light as well as on plants and animals.
Night after night our memories grow like cancer.

What did you believe in, James?
Your lines, delicate as watercolours,
strong as a hawk's talons, are marks
left on sand after the flood of your life.
What was the blackest stain?

Letter to Chris Brennan

I draw out the personal
pronoun into a long word
with its meanings collapsing
after entering a state
where confusion and corruption bubble
along together in a dangerous mood
for slip-ups, falling for Lilith again,
or Nietzsche's sour innards. *Love,*
says the round bloke,
is another form of the old pro
and that woman Bird
calls out: 'Come back, Chris!
There was never any reason to go!'
Take note, I say, there's no time
for fiddling with your keys, just open
up the bonnet, man, and show your
new idiom. These are the same
shoes, the same coat, that shirt
without a collar, fraying on both
cuffs and ink-stained – imagine
actually *eating* the ingredients
of one's breakfast!

Letter to John Tranter

In the National Library, letters you wrote
get shuffled about in a big bright cell,
each word refocussing my memory
as it hits the light, the foxed paper
loaded with concerns time's
transformed to code. Even your
black irony couldn't crack it open now,
you who told me that if I kept reading Mallarmé
I'd never make sense again. *Listen, sweet brother*
it's been a long and bloody journey
how could I wound you with the days, you wrote.
My brain 'bled truly from the broken head',
I read your poem 'Bardo Thodol' and you gave me
The Book of the Dead and laughed darkly
at the name of the doctor stuck to my
hospital bed: Lazarus. The harbour was all
around us then, our workshops projected
huge poems onto the walls of universities and kitchens.
Mallarmé is almost a brand name these days, transparency
a word politicians use to lie about the arts; in the
universities language poets write poems
in something called text. Our youthful passions
for fast cars and strange gods are played on a loop
in words recorded as sound, repeating sentimental
regrets meaning absolutely nothing.

Letter to Vicki Viidikas

We crossed Sydney Harbour from Long Nose Point,
our words trailing behind us in the wharf-shaking ferry's wake.
Killer prawns and dragonflies left phosphorous traces
behind them: everything connected.
We spoke of embracing death
to enter eternity once our bodies gave up.
Now you've done it, I can't feel 'the other side,'
unless you're back already as something
not quite human. After your funeral
I held the last poem you wrote in my
hand and felt your presence, harassing
and charming. What perverse kink
in the imagination held us back?
Maybe you were right about money,
that it was bad for poets, just like fame,
but I wanted the hit parades. You said when
we first met that your job was clipping the nails
of poodles – I thought it was some kind of joke,
but the next day met you at the 'Poodle Parlour'
and after work you bought me a copy of
Sylvia Plath's new book. One of your lines
keeps coming back: *Give up everything*
and write.

Letter to Robert Creeley

I've heard the system's closing down. It's good
reading in books, old friend, your words about
what a friend is, if you have one. These
days I often think of Zukofsky
just throwing in the word
'objectivist' and how it works
as well as any label could. These
days we're just words away
from death and I think
I've finally learnt to listen (your love
songs seem wise now that the years
have steadied my head) as you turn hurt
without sentiment to gain. I thought
of your clear humour when my father
was dying of cancer. I asked about the pain
and he spun me a line: 'it feels like a big
mud crab having a go at my spine.'

Letter to Tom Raworth

Before escaping from the clock self imposes
on the page in those days I could hardly talk
and called you in my head Tom Raw Worth,
and there was some kind of criminal in that
poem of yours called Morrell,
and the brown endpapers
of your Jonathan Cape book
were doors I slunk through. I lived
inside there, free from narrative, speaking
in a language I could see, not utter. The light
led me through chambers of murmurings, calling me,
I thought, in the pitch of your voice, though it was
streets not spires where the books were, not
blocks of stone and English holy glass, but a sly
side of the mouth code, serious song
that wouldn't parry or fuck you
for exclaiming *these lines are wonderful,*
these tough folk are not embarrassed by wonder.
Morrell's keys to the prison jingled as you walked
up walls your head took the weight
and made the weirdness surrounding me
release small change to pay for sheets of creamy Aches
that were soon transformed into a kind of folding money
so the Morrells could pay for their keys, and
on each page I made appeared that
watermark, *Raw Worth.*

Letter to Bob Dylan

You never really know who's speaking,
where the words were created or welded together,
cancelling you out. You know
what it's like to stand there though,
on the corner of some sentence
looking in at the little company with its lights,
watching the faces of the letters.
There's a crack in each memory
where, looking in, you see yourself
stuttering over the syllables, that
false smile aching the brain –
the one with a wife in its talk
who can't escape endless yammering,
or find the impossible exit from that family
forever arriving in waves, flowering
in its shell. We know how to create luck –
though it doesn't paint the final picture
with the log fire burning and the books
fat on their shelves, the cat sitting snug
with its glued-up eye. I'll leave
this letter unposted – better you
find it by telepathy. It'll arrive
as a wince or little black chuckle,
or as a faint snatch of song perhaps
praising your singing – the one thing exempt
from the tax of memory and living out the days.

The flow-through
(for the Johns)

We loved the front, your wall of words,
and the fact that snatches made
sense to the professors. We read
The Double Dream of Spring
and argued fiercely about whether
this was the way to go, tied knots
in your tangles, tendrils of phrases
that wound their way round our pages.
Those were the days we exist in now –
when we hacked through time
and came out twisted. Gaping holes
in space, we fed on sentences stitched
together with a grammar that was streetwise,
though with impeccable manners that always
got us through the gates. The mix of sweetness
and a ferocity that could burn holes
was what I admired most in *Some Trees* –
those poems were places I made friends in.
I remember Tranter standing in a classroom
reading them, his laughter edged with
irony and kindness. Ashbery days,
when poets were drunk on code within code,
when language cracked open and showed us
the power of whimsy and a dark abyss
that said 'perhaps' as it echoed.

Fishing in a landscape for love

This is swamp land, its mountains
worn down by the wings of kingfishers
flying back to their nests. Crows
are black feathers

saving me from morning.
I talk to them as if we're friends,
they look at me sideways.
When I offer them fish they eat it.

Swamp harriers whistle as they do
slow circles through the azure –
let's talk about the azure,
descriptions of place

can't imitate the legs of prawns
moving gently in the tide
from which the azure takes on meaning.
I put them into a mosquito-wire cage

and lower them from the jetty,
they jump from their sleep
at the dark of the moon.
Bait is all that matters here –

love's worn down into sound
and is contained in what I say,
these dead words feeding on live ones,
these ideas thrown to the crows –

they don't come back,
love needs live bait,
it doesn't behave
like a scavenger.

Harriet and Mary

Who knows what Shelley thought would
happen after he made love with Mary?
Before he finally left her, Harriet
made his nights terrible with grief.

Still leaving after all this time, young men read
Shelley's poems and repeat his life: how
much pain can love take and take
before it peaks on meaning?

Tonight I listen to an owl singing
in the stillness and think of it
tearing the throat out of some small animal,
making a meal of it – meaningless, brief.

Cornflowers

There are no cornflowers here –
the sunlight slants through
the glass, the harbour
glitters, ruffled by a light
westerly. The jacaranda tree
is in flower and almost
comes through the open
window. Honeysuckle
perfume, channel-billed
cuckoos and huge fruit bats
come with night – in the darkness
neon signs throwing red and blue
reflections across the surface
of the tide. Sydney Harbour Bridge
is a dark arch with lights blooming.
I pick up the empty vase and place it
on the table, knowing that when you
enter the room, it will be filled
with the missing flowers.

Flannel flowers for Juno

We walk along a crumbling bush track,
the full moon dropping through gums,
down through the sparse limbs,
their shredded bark hanging by balance –
thinking in fragments.

The air's damp and sweet.

The sounds of the river are softened
while you carry the rest of the world in your head
and I empty myself of memories one
word at a time.

They sink behind us onto the floor of the bush.

Your face shines with competence,
your hair flows, I hold your warm hand as we walk.
It feels miraculously alive compared to my
dry mouthings.

Whatever we pass by seems very old.
Twigs petrified into black glass crack under our feet.
A tawny frogmouth owl looks at us from a dead branch
unblinking, immobile, eternal.

I can't ask you for forgiveness.
Words aren't part of this landscape.
The weight of what I've done grinds away at my knees,
the joints of my bones scrape away the word 'jelly.'
My head floats on the path beside you, its hair
speckled pollen from flowering gums.

You turn to gaze into a sandstone cave.

Above the entrance, flannel flowers
grow from the roots of an ancient fig,
their blossoms closed against the dark.

Juno & Eurydice

Our boat hits the warm air sitting in Mooney Creek
as the first light of dawn begins to trace dark mountains.
We come in from the night, leaving behind
our particular hells. Back up the creek
the mist rises in great white banks –
ahead of us, our house on the point.

Each year we make it through and time brings
images and poems to map the journey –
each year we find this place holding us back
from going, the river country taking us in.
We claim it just by being here, on the brink
of darkness. A crimson rosella draws a line

of colour across the white bay: we are drenched in light
and the rich smell of the river rising from mangroves.
A welcome swallow skims the fresh water in our pool.
I couldn't live without you now, though in dreams I've
betrayed Eurydice. Death has become
a part of what the river's taught me –

this world is created for us above ground,
where even lyre birds walk slowly through your
garden holding their lyres high. We move in and out of
the myths, becoming figures from them – maybe the longer
we live here the less they matter, as we tell ourselves
stories that were here before myth.

Reading Georg Trakl

(for Garry Shead)

The lovers gaze darkly at each other
radiant in the afternoon's dimness
arms resting gently over shoulders
eyes reflecting the rich light

Beyond the black outline of the bush
a thousand birds rustle in the branches
Inside your grandmother lights the kerosene lamp
setting loose its shadows

Quite near to the house heavy fruit drops softly
onto the uncut grass in the yard
A breeze blows out the lamplight
as you turn from the map on your canvas

and listen to the surf rolling the sand back
onto the beach at Bundeena
You stay up all night waiting for sunlight
and watch as the lovers dissolve with dawn

Eurydice in Sydney

What was he thinking while I was gone?
Was his brain still doing time in his head,
dancing in abstract darkness?

Pain comes and goes. I notice things
I hadn't before: the city ibis stitching its voice
to the wind between the carpark and George Street.

I think of going shopping with him.
Bogong moths in a shaft of sunlight
flutter beneath the blue trees

of a shadowy Hyde Park. Does
Sydney Harbour still exist? depends
on how his voice murmurs

late into night as he drinks, rustling
still with that old ardour, trailing
ribbons of smoke and blood.

Mulberry leaves

Out the back in the kitchen, my mother
chops through root vegetables, filleting mullet,
threading our meals together. My father stokes
a fire in the yard, boiling up offal and fish frames
in a forty-four gallon drum; a mist rises from his
liquid fertiliser baked all day in the sun,
clinging to us and the windless air.

The heat hangs around after dark.
Steam fogs the glass of a pressure lamp
hissing yellow light from a fragile mantle.
The country music station plays softly.

Dad sings along with Hank Williams as he works.
He takes a slug of his home brew and coughs
until he lights another smoke. My hands
are full of mulberry leaves and silkworms,
the yellowish cocoons seeping transparent
blood from injured larvae. Inside my
cardboard shoe box, God laughs on.

NEW POEMS
(2004)

The first chance was the last chance

(for Sasha Grishin & Garry Shead)

Down sandstone steps to the jetty; always
the same water, lights scattered across the tide.
Remember we say, the first time.
Our eyes locked into endless permission;

this dark gift; why can't I let go
and be the man in your life, not the one who writes
your name down for the dedication page;
whatever the name, you know who I write for;

you know how private, how utterly selfish
the muses are. This is your image,
crafted in the long hours away from you.
The house rocks, money comes and goes, fish

jump against the tide, the children grow
and go out into the world. The bleak eye turns,
my tongue speaks with ease; it's the rudder
that steers the stream of words into their daily meanings –

not the meaning beyond words. I cried out
when you were not here, I smashed my fist against a stone.
My art was stone. A red glow cracked the kitchen window,
I carved the roast and served it to the cats.

Sign posts point the way, bitter laughter
stings the wounds, my black heart beats. This way
to the shop and gallery in the ordinary day. Clap
your hands against my ears, turn off the light –

you stay. It is always you, shapes change,
the music becomes a pool of melancholy sea water
distilled in sun, slapping rocks. This love
makes the art that walks in a son and moves a daughter;

they cannot always see. You can't see what makes
a spark in me – the seagull's eye reflects a shoal
of whitebait, alive with death. We move through time –
I sing in the light: the first chance was the last chance.

The dollarbird

As the family listened to the reading of the will
dollarbirds were landing, summer migrants
thudding into soft magnolia trees in bloom. It seems
I'll be able to free this captive life
in my mind, let it fall from my eyes like fish scales
and walk away; now that she'll be looked after
financially at least. These blunt threats,
the bully my conscience keeps honing daily.
How much freedom will she take?
No more lozenges of grief in brown paper bags.
I'll scatter rotten fruit on the terrace
and every flying insect on the northern peninsula
will loop and hum in droves for the feast.
Dollarbirds will hawk for them in the translucent air.
She glides through my thoughts reading
The Divine Comedy in the compartment I've filed her in:
bad? Sure, there's more housework
to be done in my mind today. Pawpaws rot
efficiently, they attract pests from miles away.
Hovering and crawling. As she listens her cheeks glow,
her thoughts swerve as elegantly
as dollarbirds gathering the words to strike.
There's a cavil, a hiccup and a shudder
down her spine. Thirty years of gibberish, resentments
drenched in perfume, years of love
and an inkling I could be wrong. Can I siphon off
the fertilising fantasy and let passion wither like old skin?
Unpleasant metaphors vanish, migrate back
to where those green feathered beakies come from:
A dollarbird tumbles as it flies above magnolia trees in bloom.

Middle Harbour to The Heads

(for John Firth Smith)

The blocks of sandstone suspended, hanging in the air
above the Old Spit Bridge, hours painted back,
black capped terns catching chips,

we talked for fifty summers
thinking it meant something, sand sticking to sweat,
sand in our tears as voices buffet the walls of years –

children, the streaks of cloud, sails flaring
in the last afternoon light. Now slabs of colour,
the lines that shape meaning, each painting remembers

friends gone, forgotten scratches of calligraphy –
what we should have said that last time;
the way a peppercorn tree by the harbour

shakes with cicadas making their throbbing note stick.

One day I watched a huge shark swimming
across Powderworks Bay, sea-lice clung to its gills like scabs;
it almost touched the side of our boat, trailing

an old cord fishing line, it kept shaking its head,
and rolled its eye as if to take us in. Who knows what
to say at the right time? Our words

float up and dance with the currawong's fluting,
a streak of brilliant white separates us from the dead,
the cicadas wave of sound encases us

and we are one hair away from live bait;
the music of these colours glints from the surfaces.
Water makes me think of paradise, indigo as black as news.

Flag-tailed bird of paradise

*(George W. Bush instructed 'the enemy' to hold up white flags
and stand twenty metres away from their tanks, promising that
if they did, they would be spared.)*

Thought to be extinct, they are
appearing through the red mist, their white tails
waving at blunt helicopters splattering
the earth. These creatures
from paradise play dead when attacked –
they freeze, clamped to a branch,
the tiny flags of their tails
barely shimmering in broken sunlight.
They once lived in jungles
on islands in the Pacific, but haven't
been found dead there since 1958.
Some escaped to Arabia: sold to collectors
and bred in captivity, they were
taken up by zoos, kept in palaces
and inbred. Flunkies fed them
and sultans hovered about them, marvelling
at how they became extraordinary in their deformities,
their cream-coloured plumage shot
through with pale, beautiful rainbows,
their eyes enormous, pink, their tail-flags heavy –
almost too heavy to hold up, but not theirs to withhold.

The goldfinches of Baghdad

These finches are kept in
gold-plated cages and fruit boxes
covered with wire mesh, they
are used by the falcon trainers as lures
and as living ornaments singing to rich patriarchs
in their death beds. Their song is pure and melodious.
A goldfinch with a slashed throat
was the subject of masterpiece painted by an artist
in the 16th century on the back
of highly polished mother-of-pearl shell:
it burns along with the living caged birds
in Saddam's palace tonight. Feathers and flesh,
hands and wings burn; and as the sirens wail
the tongues of poets and the beaks of goldfinches burn.
The ones who cannot speak burn
along with the articulate; the creatures
who are oblivious of prayer, along with the ones
who lament to their God. Falcons on their silver chains,
and the children of the falcon trainer smother
in the smoke of burning feathers and human flesh.
We must sing or die. Singing death as our songs feed the flame.

Not a penny sonnets

Remember the "club sandwich"?'
GIG RYAN

1

The book launch with plates of water biscuits –
there's always the "club sandwich" you said. We keep
splicing letters into words, our defence –
verbal tattoos; reading aloud, using our wits
to string along an empty audience,
noting the girl driving by in her low slung Torana;
those days of ordinary defeat
digging our biros in, using a Gregory's
published before the councils made the streets –
going to funerals, throwing out old affections.
We make conversation on a bus seat –
then in a lounge at the Intercontinental, making quips,
drinking beer and double gins,
I'm talking hard but nothing seems to grip.

2

I've written my response before you even speak.
We walked onto an illuminated page
stringing along the audience, acting like freaks,
digging our biros in, filling shot glasses to the brim
of separate skins, we kept honing our beaks
on a cuttlefish bone from your baptismal swim.
Cracks? We take a bite and our teeth ache
with old affections and lost destinations.
We've been looking at the edge for three decades,
drinking hard, so we had something to blame,
remembering the days when we smoked ready-mades.
You kept demanding things impossible for me;
I've nothing left, not a penny to my name – just references,
living on Smith's Chips and lemonade

3

From the Intercontinental we scoff at luck
and flash Medicare Cards before signing anything,
letting our biros dig in. *Gone with the Wind* –
breathing conditioned air, in separate skins
with goose pimples; enjoying some anti-fashion
with enemies and friends;
then walk out onto the street and breathe the city in.
A Torana spins its back wheels
and a cloud of brown smoke hangs above the street;
she's gone. We are back outside talking,
destroying words, trying to detox –
believing nothing, especially the way we feel,
our shredded trust, limping figures dressed in skin.
Where's the club sandwich now? The life we mocked
surrounds us, we're distracted but the tide keeps coming in.

Apostlebird

The house is packed;/ he doesn't need to change the act.
JAMES McAULEY

The Angry Penguins were a sort of self-corrupting
rabble, their madrigals a dangerous magic.
Come now, it was a lark my dears.
The students called me the apostlebird for years
after my my pet. Then I actually witnessed the beast, a crucifix
in one hand, a jug of afterbirth in the other.
We snipped away their unbuttoned insolence.
It was song, a bit of jazz, a few black jokes, the odd perk
nothing sexual. I tampered with
the masks. The enemy couldn't write
a sentence, I wanted my own quiddity to float
through the halls, bumping up against
the ancient forms I knew would hold. Feathers
sprouted from the arms of a boy who played the black swan.
The atheists bought on marsupials, living props
to prove life was chaos; damn it – I may
as well have spoken up for the hazard of sin, you know
the students with distemper, protesting against a just war.
I carried a dangerous animal around hoping
it would attack some innocent being
so I could understand true guilt. My wife
had to light the bonfire on cracker night,
the flames exposed my face against a floozie's thigh,
with silk stockings, her birds of paradise
stuffed and hanging in glass cases 'as if in flight'.
The jungle followed me down the corridors of power;
sick bastards, I wanted them to confront the living beast.
I kept a world in my head, protected the family:
even a careless word might start the rot – but towards the end of it,
I weakened and closed the eyes of that sinister bird.

Black laughter

Walking straight up to the man in charge, I convinced him that I was
Canadian and that my mother was from Alaska. He said: 'It's not what you
think, it's what you do that counts.' This made no difference, except of
course to the cab driver, who turned off the meter and pulled over.
     All that was after the show. Now we are on the harbour.
     These dark nights of autumn could be wonderful:
the mystifying Japanese couples getting married over and over
could be some kind of play. Nothing is what it
looks like whistling loudly into the breeze.
     This city is not for depressed children
from Alaska. Here we are constantly uplifted
by the dependable louts from the PM's office
throwing rocks at the incoming tide – this one
skipping is meant to be funny: at the Opera House
attendants scrub cubicles with my Canadian hex.
     It comes in handy when the moon comes up
and tugs at the chrome tables. In coffee shops
we stay open all night: you can read the news as it rolls off the presses.
How many have been arrested? Where now is the ABC? Someone's
playing The Fugs on a wavelength cops drive through
in their big V8s, its skew-whiff atmosphere
making the pigeons edgy.

Gang gang cockatoos

In the outer suburbs we pass under them, dark grey
with white stripes, in swishing fractals
of tropical vegetation, screeching metal songs,
swinging upside down, unlavish living ornaments,
not to mention very funny and beyond us.
However tremulous my tone of voice
who would believe my flickering conviction. My state
of mind is stencilled on the footpath,
my footprints identical to gang gangs' –
a crevice in my forehead, with a slash of grey,
my whole head a red hood; I smile
because things are so pleasurable in this mission,
my lightweight cotton top cool
in the humid days. The southerly each afternoon
ruffles my feathers and I actually allow
myself to chuckle out loud. Since my children
left for London, set up house in an exclusive suburb,
well? The colossal phone bill, a visit
maybe once in three years, snaps of the kids
dressed as gang gang chicks in a delightful garden,
daughter in law pecking for money,
a private school to teach them, 'hello cocky'. It's swell.
I've never used that word, just wanted to indicate
I'm familiar with the tone used in the cages
of middle America. Captivity provokes righteous anger.
It's all to do with the quality of your cage.
Gang gang women know the score, take it on the chin.
We scorn the first person singular because
at night we drift out, beyond the confines of thinking
into the wild.

Elegy
(for Arkie Deya Whiteley)

There's a fig tree, its black trunk shines in the rain;
a beach with small waves and a shark net;
music coming from a house, an exquisite guitar,
tonight there is nothing more bitter.

A white moon above the school yard,
resonating chords, fruit bats beating humid air –
seagulls slice open the body of a drowned rat
as the ebb exposes objects of the moon's haul.

A light flickers, a newspaper floats under the jetty.
Doc Watson can sound like a gentle waterfall.
The road to Taronga Zoo is incandescent tonight.
This bitter news arrives on the tide in an empty boat.

Red-necked avocet

Wading in a lake blocked off to the sea
our legs illuminated by white hot
mantles burning kerosene
in pressure lamps, it was all detail.
Could we know the avocets
were the victims? The acid
from our joint imagination billowed out
behind us, a killing wake;
we were all eyes, huge prawns
kicked up under our soles then zapped
away into weed beds; the wings
of swans fanned our pornographic desire
to eat the avocets tiny, speckled eggs.
One of the children looked
angelic because she shuddered
as we tried to feed her boiled prawns.
The fire on the sand crackled
with dead bulrush canes, spat whizzing
popcorn-sized embers, its flames
dancing in the darkness of the black of the moon;
our cotton clothes soaked up the taste
of the smoke's breath; we were drunk with
salt and sand; killing things,
eating seafood, talking rubbish, having fun.
Avocets migrating from our thoughts
into our words and skidding with sound as they
became human acts.

Major Mitchell's pink cockatoo

In the Malley, dodging the crooked branches
of mulga trees, she waits like a sundial,
for our caravan. Her voice a distinct falsetto
good bait for passion police or mynahs.
Time the cracker keeps her harmful, her sweat
a fixative, printing alluring shadows
on skin, sketches intricate with pain.
We track her by the dark tan wicker work
the winds make of her nests.
She is neither bird nor feathered tease of her flock,
the world crumbles into red sand
as she takes my place, I walk out prepared
to let fall; look, my frame, tail-shaped, fanning air
getting nowhere.

Thinking of Eurydice at midnight

where the light struck
HD

My Siamese cat's left a brown
snake, its back broken, on my desk.
The underground throbs outside my window.
The black highway of the river's crinkled by a light
westerly on its last legs. I want to give praise
to the coming winter, but the problem
of belief flares and buckles under
the lumpy syntax. The Unelected
President's on the radio again,
laying waste to the world.

Faith – that old myth. I drag up
impossible meanings and double divisions
of love and betrayal, light and dark. Eurydice.
Where on earth am I after all these years?
A possum eats crusts on the verandah,
standing up on its hind legs.
My weakness can't be measured.
My head contains thousands of images –
slimy mackerel splashing about in the murk.
My failures slip through fingers pointed
at the best night of my life. This one.

The cold mist falls, my head floats in the stream
of thinking. Eurydice. Did I fumble? Maybe
I was meant to be the moon's reflection,
and sing darkness like the nightjar.
Why wouldn't I detest this place, where the
sun shines on settlers and their heirs
and these heirlooms I weave
from blond silk?

The red-bearded bee-eater

The swinging gate to the forest
was a rickey affair, its hinges
sang to the ratchet-throated
bower birds, the atmosphere was
thousands of years thick,
I pushed on through
the crumbling day; green wings
opened but I was already
astray, the surf thumped against a beach
nearby, children scrambled
around pulling on wires
as a great mechanical bird flapped
on the dusty track. Then a monk
walked out of the bush
and handed out a pair of gloves
ordering me to start pulling weeds.
Sure I'm having a drink:
by dark, however, no oblivion –
my head's a burning hell
in this paradise of ferns and birds.
My wife and children carried me up
into the house. I woke
at dawn and walked about alive,
then opened the bathroom cupboard –
a bare wall at its back.
There was a crumbling hole
the red-bearded bee-eater had drilled out
a hollow for its nest: two chicks
rolled their big heads and squawked for bees.

Rainbow bee-eaters

(for Juno)

Their wings fuelled
by a knowledge of bees,
turning on axles of air;
each crescent beak
delicately coloured,
a scissor-powered talis.
Once snowy-headed
elders, gathering
honeybags of nectar
from their turpentine
forest, feathery blurs
eating ochre-fat bees.
They rise, hovering
miracles, straight up
from ancient cliffs.
Your flashlight too
exposing them:
transparencies to stay
love – film stretched
catching days – pages,
the translucent calligraphy
of their wings.

The grey whistler

There is a man knocking on the door;
he was once a friend, these days
he's on his last legs and makes a living
serving writs and collecting debts.
Samples of deliverance are considered
by the jurists as I detail my shame.
This attempt to take apart forgiveness
can be illustrated by drawing, for example
a tropical whistler. Once called the brown
whistler, it lives in mangrove swamps
and their adjoining rain forests outside
Port Keats in the Northern Territory.
This bird creates hatches in dense foliage,
one can reach into these and grapple
with the texture of human sorrow;
the thinner it becomes the more it powers
an ability to start again. Scratch
tiny black pieces from memory and then
take some lace from one of the lines
from our friend the belle-lettriste's sonnet,
use a pattern created by that Italian designer
with one eye, the one who made
his name and fortune in Paris, turn it into
a hood and I'll pull it over my head.
There's a good girl, I'm a husk if you even
wince. After all, this is the city
not some northern mangrove swamp.
The man outside knocking has a swatch of paper
he wants me to sign: tell him all I said
was 'jute' to take the onus off the conversation
he wants to have. Listen to the clamour
as the street children dismantle
his clapped-out Falcon. In the backyard
lemon tree, where the remnants
of the Japanese lantern flutter, there's a city crow,
coughing up its lungs. That old friend
knocking so persistently, as the night goes on,
becomes the grey whistler.

Brahminy kite

Humidity envelopes my boat, black mould
covers its trim, mullet gut stains
on the seats. Tide floods in across the mudflats,
small black crabs play their fiddle-claw
with a feeble left bow, day in, night out.
My hand swoops to catch a lure;
talons pierce scales and sink into a heart.

We only come to know what's at the core
of each other gradually, almost decades,
until compressed midnights
flower – black roses in sandy-eyed dawns,
all stowed to starboard, up where
the Brahminy's wings catch first light.
How did we manage it, sailing on – weathering

leagues of years; a far cry from beating
wings and the arched neck
of poetry's exhausted myths. Now
fields of light, dolphin fish skittering
around the markers, slicing apart an oily sea.
The swell's escalator takes us over the top
into a world of white crests and gull-squawk.

Off Flint & Steel, the kite hits a thermal,
then lifts into a double rainbow
stained with sailfish blood and slime –
its beaked head fits over my face.
Feel the salt spray sting my eyes, catch a glint
of fish scales in the murk beyond all tiredness,
these wings cutting on through the salt-thick atmosphere.

Eclectus parrot

Bright green, scarlet-bellied, black-billed bird
crash lands in a campsite, a fire
burning cubs' fingers, the scout master flicking
the billy with a switch and growling, smoke
billowing, turning brown.

This picture-on-a-biscuit-tin is being painted
as we read, the politician as artist
on his weekend fishing trip – his son
hammers the billy with a triangle –

thousands of budgerigars wheel across low sky:
the whole jumbles put together from used landscapes
garnished with ascending raptors.

The Minister for Defence takes his part
in this amateur ornithology –
he mimics the eclectus parrot, his face turns red
reminding us of its satin breast, and that black beak
genetically engineered for speech.

The ruff

It's difficult to describe the ruff,
this bird's a living metaphor;
puffing plumage into simile. A ruff
attempt at meaning, although a water bird,
it dances on shore. Its colour, sepia,
cream and specks of red: these tones
bleed well for watercolourists –
a cock ruff in display looks top-heavy
often toppling into absurdity.

Ruff's a word from the 16th century.
Its feathers goffered for ornamental sex.
Ritual is human. These cock birds
blow up by instinct. Ruff music,
strutting to get across how inhuman they are;
how utterly bird. They dance in lines,
you could say a feather's cadence,
if heard, may sound the ruff's dance,
a puffed pose, its head hidden by a dark cowling

and the eyes blinded by display.
The ruff's ways delight us if we have a sense
of humour or a dash of madness,
the way of the ruff is for folk
who take themselves too seriously.
The bird's habits contradict words, art
and human silence. The ruff exists on the fringes
of existence, the edges of a word's meaning
spoken in this country. Ruff.

INDEX

Index of titles and first lines

(Titles are shown in italics, first lines in roman type.)